Plain English for Lawyers

Plain English for Lawyers

SIXTH EDITION

Richard C. Wydick
LATE OF UC DAVIS SCHOOL OF LAW

Amy E. Sloan
PROFESSOR OF LAW AT UNIVERSITY
OF BALTIMORE SCHOOL OF LAW

CAROLINA ACADEMIC PRESS
Durham, North Carolina

Library of Congress Cataloging-in-Publication Data

Names: Wydick, Richard C., author. | Sloan, Amy E., 1964– author.
Title: Plain English for lawyers / Richard C. Wydick and Amy E. Sloan.
Description: Sixth edition. | Durham, North Carolina : Carolina Academic
    Press, LLC, [2019] | Includes bibliographical references and index.
Identifiers: LCCN 2018047427 | ISBN 9781531006990 (alk. paper)
Subjects: LCSH: Legal composition.
Classification: LCC KF250 .W9 2019 | DDC 808.06/634—dc23
LC record available at https://lccn.loc.gov/2018047427

e-ISBN 978-1-5310-0700-3

Carolina Academic Press, LLC
700 Kent Street
Durham, North Carolina 27701
Telephone (919) 489-7486
Fax (919) 493-5668
www.cap-press.com

Printed in the United States of America

R.C.W.
To JJW, with love

A.E.S.
To MM, ACMS, and JWMS, with love

Contents

Preface and Acknowledgments, Sixth Edition

Richard Wydick made *Plain English for Lawyers* a classic book for teaching clear legal writing. Professor Wydick passed away in 2016. I am honored to have the opportunity to revise and update the book.

My goal with the sixth edition is to continue Professor Wydick's vision of offering a concise, practical guide to clear legal writing. This edition retains the earlier editions' essential character. Readers familiar with the book will find that its structure and approach are similar to those of earlier editions—with some timely changes to keep it relevant to the writing challenges lawyers and law students face today. Those readers new to the book will find that it contains practical advice and exercises, making it an excellent choice as an instructional text, writing supplement, or resource for self-directed efforts to improve your writing.

Classic features, including chapters on omitting surplus words, using verbs to express action, and favoring active voice, remain in the book. Material from earlier editions on word choice and language quirks has been reorganized and updated. Although the techniques covered in the book apply in almost any writing context, the book has less emphasis on strategies uniquely suited to transactional or legislative drafting. The material on punctuation has been divided into two chapters, and a new chapter on document design has been added.

Each chapter contains a mix of time-tested and new exercises students can use for self-assessment by comparing their answers with the answer key in the book's Appendix. The chapters on punctuation include short exercises for each rule addressed, along with a comprehensive exercise at the end of each chapter.

Clear writing is a skill that can be learned. It isn't easy, but with instruction and practice, anyone can learn to be a better writer. *Plain English for Lawyers* is a tool for learning and practicing techniques for clear legal writing.

The sixth edition would not have been possible without the help of many people. I am indebted to Eric Easton, Dionne Koller, Kathleen Elliott Vinson, Ruth Anne Robbins, Derek Kiernan-Johnson, and James Beslity for comments on the manuscript. Linda Edwards deserves special thanks for her valuable contributions to the organization and content of the sixth edition. My library colleagues at the University of Baltimore School of Law, especially Adeen Postar and Joanne Colvin, helped me locate source material. Genevieve Hornik provided research support. I want to recognize Dean Ronald Weich and the University of Baltimore School of Law for generous support of this project. Many people at Carolina Academic Press were instrumental in the revision, including Keith Sipe, Carol McGeehan, Linda Lacy, Jennifer Hill, and Elizabeth Ebben. My family was the source of ongoing encouragement and inspiration.

Most especially, I would like to thank the Wydick family, particularly Professor Bruce Wydick, for the opportunity to work on the book and the support they gave me.

Amy E. Sloan
January 2019

Preface and Acknowledgments, Fifth Edition

The first edition of *Plain English for Lawyers* was a revised version of an article that appeared in 66 California Law Review 727, published by the students of the University of California, Berkeley, School of Law, copyright 1978, by the California Law Review, Inc.

Many of the changes made in subsequent editions reflect the ideas, writings, and suggestions made by others who toil in the field of legal writing. My debts to them are so many that to acknowledge all of them properly in footnotes or endnotes would distract the reader — a sin that all of us in the field preach against. Thus, let me here thank my scholarly creditors including the following: Kenneth Adams, Mark Adler, Robert Benson, Norman Brand, Robert Chaim, Robert Charrow, Veda Charrow, Martin Cutts, Robert Eagleson, J.M. Foers, Bryan Garner, Tom Goldstein, George Hathaway, Margaret Johns, Joseph Kimble, Philip Knight, Jethro Lieberman, Ray Parnas, Janice Redish, Peter Tiersma, Richard Thomas, and Garth Thornton. Thanks also to Keltie Jones for her fine work on the punctuation chapter.

I owe special thanks to David Mellinkoff, who died on the last day of the 20th century. He was educated at Stanford University and Harvard Law School. After serving as an artillery officer in World War II, he became a successful practicing lawyer in Beverly Hills and later a beloved law professor at UCLA. All of us in the field of legal writing have benefitted from his careful scholarship and wise guidance expressed in *The Language of the Law* (1963), *Legal Writing: Sense & Nonsense* (1982), and Mellinkoff's *Dictionary of American Legal Usage* (1992).

Richard C. Wydick
Davis, California
June 2005

Plain English for Lawyers

Why Plain English?

We lawyers do not write plain English. We use eight words to say what we could say in two. We use arcane phrases to express commonplace ideas. Seeking to be precise, we become redundant. Seeking to be cautious, we become verbose. Our sentences twist on, phrase within clause within clause, glazing the eyes and numbing the minds of our readers. The result is a writing style that has, according to one critic, four outstanding characteristics. It is "(1) wordy, (2) unclear, (3) pompous, and (4) dull."[1]

Criticism of legal writing is nothing new. In 1596, an English chancellor decided to make an example of a particularly long-winded document filed in his court. The chancellor first ordered a hole cut through the center of the document, all 120 pages. Then he ordered that the person who wrote it should have his head stuffed through the hole, and the unfortunate fellow was led around to be exhibited to all those attending court at Westminster Hall.[2]

When the common law was transplanted to America, the writing style of the old English lawyers came with it. In 1817 Thomas Jefferson lamented that in drafting statutes his fellow lawyers were accustomed to "making every other word a 'said' or 'aforesaid' and saying everything over two or three times, so that nobody but we of the craft can untwist the diction and find out what it means. . . ."[3]

Legal writing style long remained a subject of jokes and ridicule, but a reform movement started in the 1970s. A few legislatures

3

passed laws that require documents such as insurance policies and consumer contracts to be written in plain language, meaning with common words and clear phrasing that readers can understand the first time through. Banks, manufacturers, and other businesses discovered that documents written in plain language can reduce costs and increase profits. For example, an automaker's clearly written warranty can help sell cars, and a lender's clearly written loan agreement can reduce costly defaults and foreclosures. Understandable government regulations and forms have similar benefits. They can reduce the amount of staff time spent answering questions from puzzled citizens.

The movement toward plain legal language is changing the legal profession itself. Most law schools now teach the plain language style in their legal writing courses. Court rules, such as the Federal Rules of Appellate Procedure, have been rewritten to make them easier for lawyers and judges to use. Congress requires federal agencies to use plain language in drafting documents.[4] Diligent committees of experts are rewriting pattern jury instructions to help make legal doctrines understandable to the jurors who must apply them. Practicing lawyers become eager students in continuing legal education courses that teach clear writing.

Our profession has made progress, yes, but the victory is not yet won. Too many law students report from their first jobs that the plain language style they learned in law school is not acceptable to the older lawyers for whom they work. Too many estate planning clients leave their lawyer's office with a will and trust agreement in hand, but without fully understanding what they say. Too many people merely skim, or even ignore, the impenetrable paragraphs of securities disclosures, credit card agreements, apartment leases, cell phone contracts, and promissory notes, preferring to rely on the integrity or mercy of the author rather than to struggle with the author's legal prose. When was the last time you read the terms of service for a website or app? If the answer is "never," you're not alone.

Sometimes we hear amusing stories about dense notices that people neither read nor understand. For example, shoppers signed away their immortal souls in a vendor's software license. A wi-fi provider included a provision in its terms of service requiring users to pay with their first-born children.[5] Humor aside, the real-life consequence when readers cannot make sense of their legal obligations can be costly.[6]

The premise of this book is that good legal writing should not differ, without good reason, from ordinary well-written English.[7] As a well-known New York lawyer told the young associates in his firm, "Good legal writing does not sound as though it had been written by a lawyer."

In short, good legal writing is plain English. Some characteristics of plain English include:

- eliminating unnecessary words;
- choosing common, everyday words when possible;
- arranging words for clarity;
- preferring active voice;
- avoiding overly long sentences; and
- using easy-to-read design techniques.

Here is an example of plain English, the statement of facts from the majority opinion in *Palsgraf v. Long Island Railroad Co.*,[8] written by Benjamin Cardozo:

Plaintiff was standing on a platform of defendant's railroad after buying a ticket to go to Rockaway Beach. A train stopped at the station, bound for another place. Two men ran forward to catch it. One of the men reached the platform of the car without mishap, though the train was already moving. The other man, carrying a package, jumped aboard the car, but seemed unsteady as if about to fall. A guard on the car, who had held the door open, reached forward to help him in, and another guard on the platform pushed him from behind. In this act, the package was dislodged and fell upon the rails. It was a package of small size, about fifteen inches long, and was covered by newspaper. In fact it contained fireworks, but there was nothing in its appearance to give notice of its contents. The fireworks when they fell exploded. The shock of the explosion threw down some scales at the other end of the platform many feet away. The scales struck the plaintiff, causing injuries for which she sues.

What distinguishes the writing style in this passage from that found in most legal writing?

Notice Justice Cardozo's economy of words. He does not say "despite the fact that the train was already moving." He says, "though the train was already moving."

Notice his choice of words. He uses no archaic phrases, no misty abstractions, no hereinbefore's.

Notice his care in arranging words. No wide gaps appear between the subjects and their verbs or between the verbs and their objects. No ambiguities leave us wondering who did what to whom.

Notice his use of verbs. Most of them are in the simple form, and all but two are in the active voice.

Notice the length and construction of his sentences. Most of them contain only one main thought, and they vary in length: the shortest is six words, and the longest is 27 words.

These and other elements of plain English style are discussed in this book. But you cannot learn to write plain English by reading a book. You must practice these principles for yourself. That is why practice exercises are included throughout this book. When you finish a section, work the exercises. Then compare your results with those suggested in the Appendix at the end of the book.

CHAPTER TWO

Omit Surplus Words

Soon after law school, Professor Wydick was assigned to assist an experienced lawyer. The lawyer hated verbosity. When reviewing what Professor Wydick thought was a finished piece of work, the lawyer would read it quietly and take out his pen. As Professor Wydick watched, the lawyer would strike out whole lines, turn clauses into phrases, and turn phrases into single words. One day at lunch, Professor Wydick asked the lawyer how he did it. He shrugged and said, "It's not hard — just omit the surplus words."

This Chapter contains examples of surplus words and phrases. Keep them in mind and avoid them in your own writing. This Chapter also uses grammar rules to explain the functions of certain surplus words. Understanding these functions will help you spot and avoid surplus words.

How to Spot Bad Construction: Working Words and Glue Words

Every English sentence contains two kinds of words: working words and glue words. The working words carry the meaning of the sentence. In the preceding sentence the working words are these: *working, words, carry, meaning,* and *sentence.* The others are glue words: *the, the, of,* and *the.* The glue words perform a vital service. They hold the working words together to form a proper, grammatical sentence.[1] Without them, the sentence would read like a tweet. But if the *proportion* of glue words is too high, that is a symptom of a badly constructed sentence. The extra glue words add unnecessary bulk and bog down your writing.

A well-constructed sentence is like fine cabinetwork. The pieces are cut and shaped to fit together with minimal glue. When you find too many glue words in a sentence, take it apart and reshape the pieces to fit together tighter.

Consider this example:

A trial by jury was requested by the defendant.

If we underline the working words, the sentence looks like this:

A <u>trial</u> by <u>jury</u> was <u>requested</u> by the <u>defendant</u>.

Five words in that nine-word sentence are glue: *a, by, was, by,* and *the.* That proportion of glue words is too high.

How can we say the same thing in a tighter sentence with less glue? First, move *defendant* to the front and make it the subject of the sentence. Second, use *jury trial* in place of *trial by jury.* The sentence thus reads:

The defendant requested a jury trial.

If we underline the working words, the rewritten sentence looks like this:

The <u>defendant</u> <u>requested</u> a <u>jury</u> <u>trial</u>.

Again, the sentence has four working words, but the glue words have been cut from five to two. The sentence means the same as the original, but it is tighter and a third shorter.

Here is another example:

The ruling by the trial judge was prejudicial error for the reason that it cut off cross-examination with respect to issues that were vital.

If we underline the working words, we have:

> The <u>ruling</u> by the <u>trial</u> <u>judge</u> was <u>prejudicial</u> <u>error</u> for the <u>reason</u> that it <u>cut</u> <u>off</u> <u>cross-examination</u> with respect to <u>issues</u> that were <u>vital</u>.

In a sentence of 24 words, 11 carry the meaning and 13 are glue. Again, the proportion of glue is too high.

Note the string of words *the ruling by the trial judge*. That tells us that it was the trial judge's ruling. Why not just say *the trial judge's ruling*? The same treatment will tighten the words at the end of the sentence. *Issues that were vital* tells us that they were vital issues. Why not say *vital issues*? Now note the phrase *for the reason that*. Does it say any more than *because*? If not, we can use one word in place of four. Likewise, *with respect to* can be reduced to *on*.

Rewritten, the sentence looks like this:

> The trial judge's ruling was prejudicial error because it cut off cross-examination on vital issues.

Here it is with the working words underlined:

> The <u>trial</u> <u>judge's</u> <u>ruling</u> was <u>prejudicial</u> <u>error</u> because it <u>cut</u> <u>off</u> <u>cross-examination</u> on <u>vital</u> <u>issues</u>.

The revised sentence uses 15 words in place of the original 24, and 10 of the 15 are working words. The revised sentence is both tighter and stronger than the original.

Consider a third example, but this time rewrite the sentence yourself:

> In many instances, insofar as the jurors are concerned, the jury instructions are not understandable because they are too poorly written.

Does your sentence trim the phrase *in many instances*? Here the single word *often* will suffice. Does your sentence omit the phrase *insofar as the jurors are concerned*? That adds bulk but little meaning. Finally, did you find a way to omit the clumsy *because* clause at the end of the sentence?

Your rewritten sentence should look something like this:

Often jury instructions are too poorly written for the jurors to understand.

Here it is with the working words underlined:

<u>Often</u> <u>jury</u> <u>instructions</u> are <u>too</u> <u>poorly</u> <u>written</u> for the <u>jurors</u> to <u>understand.</u>

The rewritten sentence is nine words shorter than the original, and eight of its 12 words are working words.

➤ Exercise 1

Underline the working words in the sentences below. Note the proportion of glue words to working words. Next, rewrite the sentences, underline the working words, and compare your results with the original sentences. Then look at the exercise key in the Appendix.

1. In point of fact 350 grams of J-12 plastic explosive, seven detonating devices, and one 50-foot roll of insulated copper wire were discovered by the federal security inspectors at the airline gate hidden on the accused's person at the time he was detained and arrested.

2. There is nothing in the loan agreement, as we read its terms and conditions, that could be construed to allow prepayment of the loan by the borrower and simultaneous termination of the City's equity share. Prepayment of the loan will not affect the City's equity share, which will remain due upon either the sale of the property in question or upon the occurrence of any of the breaches specified in said loan agreement.

3. When entering into an agreement regarding the settlement of a claim made by a client, a lawyer must not offer or agree to a

provision that imposes a restriction of the right of the lawyer to practice law, including the right to undertake representation of or take particular actions on behalf of other clients or potential clients with similar claims.

Avoid Compound Constructions

Compound constructions use three or four words to do the work of one or two words. They suck the energy from your writing. Many excess glue words are compound prepositions and compound subordinating conjunctions.

Both prepositions and conjunctions are, by definition, glue words because they connect parts of a sentence. Prepositions connect nouns and pronouns to the rest of a sentence. Conjunctions connect like items, as in "bread *and* butter." A subordinating conjunction connects a dependent clause to an independent clause, as in this example: "The judge will stay the proceedings *if the parties agree to mediation.*" Here, *if the parties agree to mediation* is a dependent clause, and *if* is a subordinating conjunction. (If these terms are unfamiliar, you may want to review the definitions in Chapter 8.)

You saw some examples of compound constructions in the last section. *With respect to* was used instead of the preposition *on. For the reason that* was used instead of the subordinating conjunction *because.*

Every time you see one of these pests on your page, swat it. Grammar checking software may flag compound constructions for you. You can spot many of them yourself by watching for noun sandwiches: *preposition*-noun-*preposition* and *preposition*-noun-*that* phrases. One or two words will often do instead. For example, the noun sandwich *by*-means-*of* is a compound preposition that can be shortened to *by.* Another, *in*-the-event-*that,* can be shortened to the subordinating conjunction *if.*

Here is a list of examples:

COMPOUND	SIMPLE
by means of	by
by reason of	because of
by virtue of	by, under
for the purpose of	to
in accordance with	by, under
inasmuch as	since, because
in connection with	with, about, concerning
in favor of	for
in order to	to
in relation to	about, concerning
in the event that	if
in the nature of	like
on the ground that	because
prior to	before
subsequent to	after
with a view to	to
with reference, regard, respect to	about, concerning, regarding, respecting

➤ Exercise 2

Use one or two words to replace the compound constructions in these sentences. Then look at the exercise key in the Appendix.

1. For the purpose of controlling how his art collection could be displayed subsequent to his death, the doctor created a very restrictive trust with a view to keeping everything exactly as it was during his lifetime.

2. In relation to the enormous charitable gift deduction claimed by the taxpayer, inasmuch as she failed to submit an appraiser's report with reference to the donated bronze sculpture, we pro-

pose to disallow the deduction in accordance with the Revenue Department's standard operating procedure.

3. The relief sought by plaintiff in connection with this case is in the nature of a mandatory injunction. Prior to the merger of law and equity, only a court of Chancery could grant such relief.

4. In order to raise funds, the charity's organizers held a silent auction on the ground that a game of chance would not be permitted by virtue of state gaming law.

Avoid Word-Wasting Expressions

Once you develop a distaste for surplus words, you will start to notice many word-wasting expressions that appear commonly in legal writing. You can trim them from your sentences with no loss of meaning.

One of the worst offenders is *the fact that*. Consider this example:

The fact that the defendant was young may have influenced the jury.

What meaning does *the fact that* add? Why not say:

The defendant's youth may have influenced the jury.

The fact that is almost always surplus. To make sense, *fact* must be connected to something. Which fact? The fact *that the defendant was young*. You can shorten your sentence by simply stating the relevant fact. Here are some examples of alternatives to *the fact that*:

VERBOSE	CONCISE
the fact that she had died	her death
he was aware of the fact that she had died	he knew that she had died he knew about her death
despite the fact that she had died	despite her death although, even though she had died
because of the fact that she had died	because of her death because she had died

Likewise, words like *case, instance,* and *situation* spawn verbosity. They can often be replaced by shorter alternatives:

VERBOSE	CONCISE
in some instances the parties can	sometimes the parties can
in many cases you will find	often, frequently you will find
In the majority of instances the grantor will	usually, normally, generally the grantor will
that was a situation in which the court	there the court
disability claims are now more frequent than was formerly the case	disability claims are more frequent now
injunctive relief is required in the situation in which	injunctive relief is required when

Other examples of common word-wasting expressions that you can shorten with no loss of meaning are:

VERBOSE	CONCISE
a number of	some, several, a few, many
a sufficient number of	enough
an amount of	(omit and start with the number)
at that point in time	then
at this point in time	now
during the time that	during, while
for the period of	for
on a [daily, weekly, monthly, annual, yearly] basis	daily, weekly, monthly, annually, yearly
there is no doubt but that	doubtless, no doubt
until such time as	until

➤ Exercise 3

Revise these examples to omit the word-wasting expressions and other surplus words. Then look at the exercise key in the Appendix.

1. Because of the fact that parties in many instances can find a sufficient number of points of agreement to resolve a lawsuit before trial, there is no doubt but that mediation can be effective in reducing the backlog of pending cases.

2. At such time as the court issues a scheduling order, the case will proceed to discovery.

3. Subsequent to the court's ruling, the defendants filed a notice of appeal.

4. This is a situation in which mandatory injunctive relief is inappropriate.

5. Despite the fact that at this point in time the statute of limitations has passed, the plaintiff just filed a complaint alleging negligence.

6. Commencement of construction is prohibited until such time as your plans receive the approval of the design review committee.

7. In the majority of instances, the insurance adjuster will, at the outset, deny the claim.

8. The auditors review the files on an annual basis.

9. Given the fact that the regulations are hard to understand, inspectors issue citations for violations more frequently than was formerly the case.

10. Instigation of a lawsuit in the absence of a good faith belief that the underlying claim is supported by a sound legal and factual basis can result in professional discipline of the attorney, in addition to the imposition of litigation sanctions on both the attorney and on the client as well.

Avoid *It is* Sentences

It is a wonderful word.[2] When used to refer to another noun (the antecedent), *it* makes our writing more efficient. Imagine how cumbersome and awkward our prose would sound if we repeated each noun each time we referred to that noun. But because *it* is such a versatile word, we can be tempted to use *it* in ways that make our sentences wordy and fogbound. Be alert when you find a sentence or clause that begins with *it* followed by a form of the verb *to be*. Does the *it* refer to something specific? If not, you may be wasting words. In particular, get rid of *it* in a "drum roll" phrase or as a stand-in for the real actor.

Consider this passage:

The summons arrived this morning. It is on your desk.

The second sentence begins with *it*, followed by *is*, a form of the verb *to be*. The sentence is not faulty, however, because the *it* obviously refers to the antecedent — *summons* — in the prior sentence.

But what does the *it* refer to in the following sentence?

It is obvious that the summons was not properly served.

The *it* does not refer to anything specific; rather, it points off into the fog somewhere. The *it is* phrase, which makes up almost half the sentence, is nothing more than a drum roll leading up to the real content regarding service of the summons.

The sentence should be revised to eliminate the drum roll:

The summons was not properly served.

Or, if you want to emphasize the obviousness of the error: Obviously, the summons was not properly served.

Another ineffective use of *it* is as a stand-in for the real actor. Here is an example:

It is possible for the court to modify the judgment.

It again lacks a reference to anything specific but nevertheless plays a lead role as the subject of the sentence. Without a clear antecedent, *it* cannot do anything; *it* can only be. Therefore, *it* requires the inactive verb *is* to form a grammatically correct sentence. What purpose do the first four words in the sentence serve? None. They preempt the most important position in the sentence — the beginning — where the reader wants to find the actor and the action, and they take over the most important grammatical roles. The actor (*court*), the action (*modify*) and the object (*judgment*) are relegated to supporting roles.

When you see *it* at the beginning of a sentence, ask yourself: "Who is doing what to whom in this sentence?"[3] If *it* is standing in for the true actor, rewrite the sentence to focus on the elements that should be in the lead roles — the actor, the action, and the object of the action (if there is an object). First, state the actor. Then, state the action, using the strongest verb that will fit. Last, state the object of the action, if there is an object.

The sentence is both shorter and stronger when it is rewritten this way:

The court can modify the judgment.

There creates the same sentence problems as *it* when *there* substitutes for the true actor in the sentence. Here is an example:

There were no reasons offered by the court for denying punitive damages.

The *there* points off into the fog. The actor in the sentence is *court*, but it is hidden away in the middle of the sentence. Note that *there* is followed by *were*, a form of the verb *to be*. *Were* takes the place of the verb that should carry the action (*offered*). The sentence would be shorter and stronger if it read:

The court offered no reasons for denying punitive damages.

> ➤ Exercise 4

Focus on the actor, the action, and the object (if there is one) when you rewrite these sentences. Also, omit as many surplus words as you can. Then look at the exercise key in the Appendix.

1. There are three interrelated reasons that might be the motivation for a person to make a gift of significant size to a charitable organization.

2. First, it is often primarily the case that the person is motivated by a desire to benefit the charity in question.

3. There is also the issue of avoiding the capital gains tax, which is frequently the second reason why a person might donate an asset that has sharply increased in value during the time that the person has owned it.

4. In the event that the person is exceedingly wealthy, it is possible that a third reason a large charitable donation might be made is for the purpose of reducing the amount of estate taxes due at the time of his or her death.

5. It is important for tax lawyers and estate planners to show clients the multiple ways gifts to charity can produce beneficial results at tax time.

Avoid Redundant Legal Phrases

Why do lawyers use the term *null and void*? According to the dictionary, either *null* or *void* by itself would do the job. But lawyers seem impelled to write *null and void*, as though driven by primordial instinct. Occasionally a lawyer, perhaps believing that *null and void* looks naked by itself, will write *totally null and void*, or perhaps *totally null and void and of no further force or effect whatsoever*.

The phrase *null and void* is an example of coupled synonyms — a pair or string of words with the same or nearly the same meaning.[4] Here are other common examples:

alter or change	last will and testament
confessed and acknowledged	made and entered into
convey, transfer, and set over	order and direct
for and during the period	peace and quiet
force and effect	rest, residue, and remainder
free and clear	save and except
full and complete	suffer or permit
give, devise, and bequeath	true and correct
good and sufficient	undertake and agree

Coupled synonyms have ancient roots. Some of them come from the days when lawyers in England needed to make themselves understood to both the courts (which used Latin and later law French) and to common folk (who used Old English and later Middle English).[5] For example, *free and clear* comes from the Old English *freo* and the Old French *cler*. Other coupled synonyms are alliterative, which means that the joined terms begin with the same sound, like *to have and to hold*. In the days when many legal transactions were oral, the alliteration was an aid to memory.[6] Still other coupled synonyms served a rhetorical purpose.[7] That is, they used to sound impressive, like *ordered, adjudged, and decreed*.[8] Whatever their origin, coupled synonyms became traditional in legal language, and they persist today, long after any practical purpose has died.

Ask a modern lawyer why he or she uses a term like *suffer or permit* in a simple apartment lease. The first answer will likely be: "for precision." True, *suffer* has a slightly different meaning than its companion *permit*. But *suffer* in this sense is now rare in ordinary usage, and *permit* would do the job if it were used alone.

The lawyer might then tell you that *suffer or permit* is better because it is a traditional legal term of art. Traditional it may be, but a term of art it is not. A term of art is a short expression that (a) conveys a fairly well agreed-upon meaning, and (b) saves the many words that would otherwise be needed to convey that meaning. *Suffer or permit* fails to satisfy the second condition, and perhaps the first as well.

The word *hearsay* is an example of a true term of art. First, its core meaning is well agreed upon in modern evidence law, although its meaning at the margin has always inspired scholarly debate.[9] Second, *hearsay* enables a lawyer to use one word instead of many to describe a statement that was not made by the speaker while testifying at the trial or hearing and that is being offered into evidence to prove that what it asserts is true. One word that can say all that deserves our praise and deference. But *suffer or permit* does not.

Suffer or permit probably found its way into that apartment lease because the lawyer was working from a form that had been used around the office for years. The author of the form, perhaps long dead, probably worked from some even older form that might, in turn, have been inspired by a form or some now defunct appellate case where the phrase was used but not examined.

If you want your writing to have an anachronistic feel, by all means use as many coupled synonyms as you can find. If you want it to be crisp, use few or none.[10] When one looms up on your page, stop to see if one of the several words, or perhaps a fresh word, will carry your intended meaning. You will find, for example, that the phrase *last will and testament* can be replaced by the single word *will*.[11]

This is not as simple as it sounds. Lawyers are busy, cautious people, and they cannot afford to make mistakes. The old, redundant phrase has worked in the past; a new one may somehow raise a question. The research to check it will take time, and time is the lawyer's most precious commodity. But remember — once you slay one of these old monsters, it will stay dead for the rest of your legal career. If your memory is short, keep a list of slain redundancies. Such trophies distinguish a lawyer from a scrivener.

➤ Exercise 5

In the following passage you will find all the kinds of surplus words discussed in Chapter 2. Rewrite the passage, omitting as many surplus words as you can. Then look at the exercise key in the Appendix.

It cannot be gainsaid that one of the primary obligations owed by an agent to his or her principal is to act with the degree of carefulness, competence, and diligent devotion to duty that are normally exercised by and/or employed by agents of ordinary skill and prudence in like or similar circumstances. In the situation in which the agent in question is possessed of special skills and/or knowledge, that is a factor to be taken into account in determining whether the agent in question did or did not act in accordance with the legal standard of due care and diligence. Moreover, it goes without saying that it is the duty of an agent to undertake a course of action only within the metes and bounds of the actual authority granted by the principal to the agent. It is the duty of an agent to act in compliance with all instructions that are within the bounds of the law and that are received from either the principal himself or herself or persons theretofore designated by the principal as respects actions taken by the agent for or on behalf of the principal.

Use Verbs to Express Action

At its core, the law is not abstract. It is part of a real world full of people who live and move and do things to other people. Car drivers *collide*. Plaintiffs *complain*. Judges *decide*. Defendants *pay*. To express this life and motion, a writer must use verbs — action words.

The purest verb form is the base verb, like *collide, complain, decide,* and *pay*. Base verbs are simple creatures. They cannot tolerate adornment. If you try to dress them up, you squash their life and motion. The base verb *collide* can be decked out as a noun, *collision*. Likewise, *complain* becomes *complaint. Decide* becomes *decision. Pay* becomes *payment.*

Lawyers love these words. Lawyers do not *act* — they *take action.* They do not *assume* — they *make assumptions.* They do not *conclude* — they *draw conclusions.*

A base verb that has been turned into a noun has many aliases: derivative noun, nominalization, hidden verb, and zombie noun,[1] to name just a few. No matter the label, beware of a verb in noun's clothing.[2] In this Chapter you will learn to spot derivative nouns and avoid them when base verbs will do the job.

A derivative noun is just that — a noun — and cannot carry the action in the sentence. The derivative noun thus requires a supporting verb, often an inactive verb like a form of *to be*. Derivative nouns attract weak verbs because the verb does not carry the real action of the sentence. The real action is trapped in the derivative noun. The derivative noun also frequently requires extra linking words, such as prepositions or articles, to function properly in a sentence. These are words you would not need if the real action were expressed with a verb.

If you use derivative nouns instead of base verbs, surplus words will swarm like gnats. "Please *state* why you *object* to the question," comes out like this: "Please *make a statement* of why you are *interposing an objection* to the question." The base verb *state* can do the work all alone. But to get the same work out of *statement*, you need a supporting verb (*make*), an article (*a*), and a preposition (*of*). The word *objection* attracts a similar cloud of surplus words.

You can spot derivative nouns in several ways. Look for words with these endings:

-al	-ance	-ancy
-ant	-ence	-ency
-ent	-ion	-ity
-ment		

Certain verbs can also help you spot derivative nouns. Look for any of the following verbs:

achieve	effect	give
have	make	reach
take	any form of the verb to be	

Lastly, derivative nouns frequently like to hide between an article (*a, an, the*) and the preposition *of*, as in *the consideration of* or *a payment of*.[3]

These techniques for spotting derivative nouns are guides, not precise formulas. Not all words with these characteristics are derivative nouns, and not all derivative nouns have these characteristics.

More importantly, not all derivative nouns are bad. Sometimes a derivative noun is the most efficient way to express an idea. You saw an example of this in the last Chapter. *The fact that she had died* became *her death. Death* is the noun form of the verb *die.* In the example, we used two words — *her death* — in place of six — *the fact that she had died* — to solve a wordiness problem. When you express a concept like *death, enjoyment,* or *achievement* instead of an action, you often need a derivative noun.

Although derivative nouns are helpful when used appropriately, do not overuse them. When you find one on your page, stop to see if you can make your sentence shorter and stronger by using a base verb instead. The technique described in the last Chapter can help with this task: Ask who is doing what to whom, and then make the actor the subject of the sentence. This will release the action trapped in the derivative noun so you can express it with a base verb. This technique is not a cure-all, but using it is a good start toward solving many derivative noun problems.

➤ Exercise 6

Revise these sentences, omitting surplus words and, where possible, using base verbs in place of derivative nouns. Then look at the exercise key in the Appendix.

1. The failure to obtain preapproval for medical care in many instances results in a health insurer's automatic rejection of a policyholder's claim for coverage.
2. Instead, the insurer should give careful consideration to whether the policyholder sought routine or emergency treatment.
3. The preapproval requirement does not apply to emergency treatment. The insurer's evaluation of what constitutes an emergency situation must be made on a case-by-case basis.
4. In an emergency, the policyholder has to make a quick decision to seek treatment and may not have the ability to contact the insurer.

5. A term by implication in every contract is that the parties have a duty of good faith and fair dealing, and insurance contracts are no exception.

6. Fulfillment of the duty of good faith by the insurance company has as one of its requirements an obligation to respond with coherence to a policyholder's claim for emergency care that was not preceded by a request for preapproval.

CHAPTER FOUR

Prefer the Active Voice

Active and *passive voice* are terms that describe how a sentence's verb relates to its subject and direct object. Both active and passive voice are grammatically correct sentence structures. But active voice is frequently a more effective writing choice. In this Chapter, you will learn to tell the difference between active and passive voice, use active voice to avoid wordiness and ambiguity, and recognize contexts when passive voice is appropriate.

The Difference Between Active and Passive Voice

When you use a verb in the active voice, the subject of the sentence does the acting. "John kicks the ball" is in the active voice. *John* is the subject, and John does the acting: he kicks the ball. When you use a verb in the passive voice, the subject of the sentence is acted upon. "The ball is kicked by John" is in the passive voice. *Ball* is the subject, and the ball is being acted upon: it is kicked by John.

ACTIVE   John kicked the ball.

PASSIVE   The ball was kicked by John.

Both the active voice and the passive voice can express action in various tenses, that is, action at various times. For example:

ACTIVE VOICE	PASSIVE VOICE
John kicked the ball.	The ball was kicked by John.
John kicks the ball.	The ball is kicked by John.
John will kick the ball.	The ball will be kicked by John.
John has kicked the ball.	The ball has been kicked by John.
John had kicked the ball.	The ball had been kicked by John.
John will have kicked the ball.	The ball will have been kicked by John.

No matter what the verb tense — past, present, future, or something more complicated — the key difference between the active and passive voice remains the same: in the active voice, the subject of the sentence does the acting, but in the passive voice, the subject of the sentence is acted upon.

➢ Exercise 7

First, underline the verbs in these sentences. (Note that some of the sentences have more than one verb.) Next, identify each verb as either active voice or passive voice. Then look at the exercise key in the Appendix.

1. Benson failed to renew his commercial driver's license for five years after it expired. Therefore, he was required to retake the exam to obtain a new license.

2. For more than three months after obtaining a new license, Benson sought a position as a driver. Then he caused an accident in his personal vehicle and was charged with reckless driving. He was convicted of a misdemeanor last June.

3. Last July, a new statute went into effect. It requires Benson to disclose the traffic conviction to any employer who hires him as a commercial driver.

4. Benson mistakenly believed the statute did not apply to him. He reasoned that he was not required to disclose the convic-

tion because the vehicle involved in the accident was his personal car, not a commercial vehicle.

5. Benson was hired as a commercial driver last August. Two weeks later, he was fired by his employer and cited by the police for failing to disclose the prior traffic conviction. Benson now challenges the disclosure statute's validity.

Problems with the Passive Voice: Wordiness and Ambiguity

The passive voice creates two problems. It uses more words than active voice, and it risks creating ambiguity.

Look again at an example from the last section:

ACTIVE   John kicked the ball.

PASSIVE   The ball was kicked by John.

The two sentences mean the same thing, but observe that the sentence in the passive voice is longer than the sentence in the active voice. In the active voice, the single word *kicked* expresses the action all by itself. The passive voice needs three words, *is kicked by*, to express the same action. The passive voice is wordier. Notice how, in each of the following examples, the active voice takes fewer words than the passive voice:

ACTIVE VOICE	PASSIVE VOICE
The union filed a complaint.	A complaint was filed by the union.
The trial judge will deny your motion.	Your motion will be denied by the trial judge.
The legislative history supports our conclusion.	Our conclusion is supported by the legislative history.
The trustor had not intended the trust to . . .	The trust had not been intended by the trustor to . . .

Wordiness is not the only disadvantage of the passive voice. The passive voice can also be ambiguous. With the active voice, you can usually tell who is doing what to whom. With the passive voice, however, the writer can hide the identity of the actor. That construction is called the "truncated passive." For example: "The ball was kicked." Who kicked the ball? We have no way to know; the actor is hidden in the fog of the truncated passive.

A writer who wants to befog the matter totally will couple the truncated passive with a derivative noun, like this: "A kicking action was accomplished," thus hiding both the kicker and the kickee. The truncated passive can be especially troublesome in legal writing. Consider this patent license provision:

> All improvements of the patented invention that are made hereafter shall promptly be disclosed, and failure to do so shall be deemed a material breach of this license agreement.

Who must disclose improvements to whom? Must the licensor disclose improvements it makes to the licensee? Must the licensee disclose improvements it makes to the licensor? Must each party disclose improvements it makes to the other party? If it ever becomes important to know, the parties will probably have to slug it out in a lawsuit, all because of the truncated passive voice.

When to Use the Passive Voice

Notice that the title of this Chapter says *prefer* the active voice. It *doesn't* say never use the passive voice. The passive voice has many proper uses. Passive voice is the better choice in the following circumstances:

USE PASSIVE VOICE WHEN	EXAMPLES
The thing done is important, and who did it is not.	The subpoena was served on January 19th.
You don't know who did it.	The data files were mysteriously destroyed.

You want the subject of the sentence to connect with words at the end of the preceding sentence.	The committee presented the award to Frederick Moore. Moore was arrested by the FBI the following day.
You want to place a strong element at the end of the sentence for emphasis.	When the victim walked through the door, he was shot.
A sense of detached abstraction is appropriate.	In the eyes of the law, all persons are created equal.
You want to muddy the waters.	The plaintiff's teeth were knocked out. (Use this construction if you do not want to state outright that your client knocked out the plaintiff's teeth.)

Thus, if you can articulate a good reason for using the passive voice, use it. But elsewhere, use the active voice; it will make your writing clearer and more concise.

➤ Exercise 8

Rewrite these sentences, omitting surplus words and using the active voice unless you can articulate a good reason for using the passive voice. Supply any missing information that you need. Then look at the exercise key in the Appendix.

1. The statute was enacted in 2018.
2. The bank was not notified by either the depositor or anyone else that the debit card had been stolen.
3. A financial aid application must be completed and submitted to the Financial Aid Office at least 90 days before the start of classes.

4. After 180 days, this Agreement can be terminated by either party.

5. Two kilograms of an unidentified white powder were discovered by the police in the spare tire well of the Volvo sedan.

6. Charitable gifts of appreciated assets can be deducted at their fair market value at the time of the gift, and in that way capital gains tax can be avoided by you.

7. The plaintiff was prohibited from leaving the store by the security guard; therefore, a claim for false imprisonment was filed by the plaintiff against the guard and the store owner.

CHAPTER FIVE

Use Short Sentences

Short sentences are easier to understand than long sentences. Long sentences are complex. Complexity in writing has been called "the greatest enemy of clear communication."[1] Law, however, often involves complex ideas. Figuring out how to communicate complex ideas with short, clear sentences requires skill. In this Chapter, we dissect and rewrite a long sentence to illustrate techniques you can use to write short, clear sentences.

You could be forgiven for thinking that lengthy sentences sound lawyerly. English-speaking lawyers have a long tradition of writing long, complicated sentences. The tradition began centuries ago when English writers used punctuation to guide oral delivery, rather than to help convey the meaning of a sentence.[2] In law, the tradition persisted even after writing conventions changed in ordinary English prose. When lawyers write, they tend to deliver to the reader one enormous chunk containing all their main themes, supporting reasons, details, qualifications, exceptions, and conclusions.

Although no form of legal writing is immune from this problem, statutes and regulations in particular suffer from long, convoluted sentences. Lawyers understandably desire to include all components of a rule together. Perhaps they fear that readers will rush out to violate the law unless all parts of a rule appear in one sentence. If so, the fear is unfounded. A more realistic concern is that readers will not comply with rules they cannot understand.

To prove to yourself that long sentences make legal writing hard to understand, read the following passage at your normal speed. Then ask yourself what it means.

> In a trial by jury, the court may, when the convenience of witnesses or the ends of justice would be promoted thereby, on motion of a party, after notice and hearing, make an order, no later than the close of the pretrial conference in cases in which such pretrial conference is to be held, or in other cases, no later than 10 days before the trial date, that the trial of the issue of liability shall precede the trial of any other issue in the case.

The subject matter of that passage is not profound or complicated, but the passage is hard to understand. It consists of a single sentence, 86 words long, containing five pieces of information:

1. In a jury case, the liability issue may be tried before any other issue.
2. The judge may order the liability issue to be tried first if that will serve the convenience of witnesses or the ends of justice.
3. The judge may make the order on a party's motion, after notice and hearing.
4. In a case with a pretrial conference, the judge may make the order no later than the end of the conference.
5. In a case with no pretrial conference, the judge may make the order no later than 10 days before the trial date.

The original passage is hard to understand for two reasons. First, the single-sentence format distorts the logical order of the five pieces of information. The first thing readers want to know is what this rule is about. It is about the trial of the liability issue before other issues. Before telling readers *what* the rule is about, the writer inserts the *why* (convenience or justice), the *how* (a party's motion), and the *when* (pretrial conference or 10 days before trial). Readers are not concerned about the *why, how,* and *when* of this rule before they know the *what*. The rule's objective does not appear until the last 20 words of the sentence. With another rule, you might need to place a different component first. Your goal is to present information in the order most useful to readers, and the single-sentence format often interferes with that goal.

Second, the single-sentence format tests a reader's stamina by separating the key parts of the sentence. The subject of the sentence (*court*) appears at word seven. At word 32, the verb (*make*) finally shows up. Part of the object (*an order*) comes next, but the critical description of the order's purpose remains hidden until the reader arrives, breathless, at word 68. By then the reader has forgotten the subject and verb and must backtrack through the sentence to find them.

We could rewrite this sentence to place the components in a logical order and keep the subject, verb, and object close together:

> In a jury case, the court may order the liability issue to be tried before any other issue when trying the liability issue first serves the convenience of witnesses or the ends of justice and when the order is made upon a party's motion and after notice and a hearing, as long as the court makes the order not later than the end of the pretrial conference or, in a case without a pretrial conference, 10 days before the trial date.

This version is better. The rule's objective appears at the beginning, and the subject, verb, and object are close together. But it is still a lot to absorb in a single chunk. Readers need to stop and catch their breath at several points in that sentence. Why tire them out by making them hike up a steep hill all at once? When they stop for rest, as they surely will, they may lose their place or give up reading the sentence altogether. Readers will follow the path more readily when you break the journey into manageable pieces. Instead of writing one long sentence containing five thoughts, use five sentences, each containing one thought. Here is one way to do that:

> In a jury case, the court may order the liability issue to be tried before any other issue. The court may make the order if doing so

serves the convenience of witnesses or the ends of justice. The court may make the order on a party's motion, after notice and hearing. In a case with a pretrial conference, the court may make the order no later than the end of the conference. In a case with no pretrial conference, the court may make the order no later than 10 days before the trial date.

Instead of one long sentence, we now have five sentences with an average length of 19 words. Each sentence contains only one main thought, and the thoughts follow in logical sequence.

Passages like the one above suggest a two-part guide to writing clear, understandable sentences:

1. In *most* sentences, convey only one main thought.
2. Keep the *average* sentence length below 25 words.

Do not misinterpret this guide. Part 1 says that *most* sentences should contain only one main thought. It does *not* say that *every* sentence should contain only one main thought. To keep the reader's interest, you need variety in sentence construction: some simple sentences that express only one main thought, interspersed with some compound or complex sentences that express two or more related thoughts. For example, the first two sentences above could be combined with no loss of clarity: "In a jury case, the court may order the liability issue to be tried before any other issue when doing so serves the convenience of witnesses or the ends of justice."

Likewise, Part 2 says that the *average* length of your sentences should be less than 25 words. It does *not* say that *every* sentence should be 25 words or less. You need variety in sentence length as well as sentence construction: some short sentences, some of medium length, and an occasional long one in which related thoughts are joined. (The advanced spelling and grammar settings in your word processing software should calculate average sentence length for you.)

When you include a long sentence to create rhythm in your writing, bear in mind Mark Twain's advice. Although you may occasionally indulge in a long sentence, you must construct the sentence with care: "[M]ake sure there are no folds in it, no vaguenesses, no parenthetical interruptions of its view as a whole" so that "it won't be a sea-serpent with half of its arches under the water; it will be a torch-light procession."[3]

➤ Exercise 9

Rewrite these passages using short sentences and omitting as many surplus words as you can. Then look at the exercise key in the Appendix.

1. In an action grounded upon the law of torts, an actor is not liable for harm that is different from the harms whose risks made the actor's conduct tortious, nor for harm when the tortious aspect of the actor's conduct did not increase the risk of harm, but when an actor's tortious conduct causes harm to a person that, because of the person's preexisting physical or mental condition or other characteristic, is of a greater magnitude or different type than might reasonably be expected, the actor is nevertheless liable for all such harm to the person. (96 words, average sentence length 96 words)

2. The American Bar Association, recognizing that, despite the pride Americans take in their system of trial by jury, there is room for vast improvement in the manner in which juries are selected, treated in the courtroom, instructed on the law, and compensated for their services, has adopted Principles Relating to Juries and Jury Trials, which calls for reforms, including, for example, a proposal that states that in civil cases jurors should ordinarily be permitted to submit written questions for witnesses. (80 words, average sentence length 80 words)

3. In decisions concerning the sentencing and correction of individual offenders, the general purposes of the law ought to be to render punishment within a range of severity sufficient to reflect the gravity of the offense and blameworthiness of the of-

fenders, and where there is a realistic prospect of success, to serve the goals of offender rehabilitation, general deterrence, incapacitation of dangerous offenders, and restoration of crime victims and communities, but to impose sentences no more severe than necessary to achieve the foregoing purposes. (83 words, average sentence length 83 words)

CHAPTER SIX

Arrange Your Words Carefully

Poorly arranged words can make your writing difficult for readers to understand, even when the sentence structure is grammatically correct. In this Chapter, you will learn to avoid ambiguity by paying attention to how you arrange the words in your sentences.

Avoid Wide Gaps Between the Subject, the Verb, and the Object

To make your writing easy to understand, most of your declaratory sentences should follow the normal English word order: first the subject, next the verb, and then the object (if there is one). For example:

> subject   verb
>
> The <u>defendant</u> <u>demurred</u>.

> subject   verb   object
>
> The <u>defendant</u> <u>filed</u> six <u>affidavits</u>.

In seeking to understand a sentence, the reader's mind searches for the subject, the verb, and the object. If those three key elements are set out in that order, close together, near the front of the sentence, the reader will understand quickly.

Lawyers, however, often test the agility of their readers by making them leap wide gaps between the subject and the verb and between the verb and the object. For example:

> A claim, which in the case of negligent misconduct shall not exceed $500, and in the case of intentional misconduct shall not exceed $1,000, may be filed with the Office of the Administrator by any injured party.

In that sentence, readers must leap a 22-word gap to get from the subject (claim) to the verb (may be filed). Structuring the sentence this way violates three principles you have already learned. It uses the passive voice unnecessarily, includes more than one idea, and at 37 words, is longer than most sentences should be. The best remedy for a wide gap like this one is to turn the intervening words into a separate sentence:

> Any injured party may file a claim with the Office of the Administrator. A claim must not exceed $500 for negligent misconduct or $1,000 for intentional misconduct.

Usually you can avoid wide gaps by following the principles you learned in earlier Chapters. Occasionally, however, wide gaps can still work their way into your writing. You should eliminate them whenever you find them.

Smaller gaps between subject and verb can also make your writing hard for the reader to understand. You can close these gaps by moving the intervening words to the beginning or the end of the sentence:

GAP	GAP CLOSED
This agreement, unless revocation has occurred at an earlier date, shall expire on November 1, 2025.	Unless revoked sooner, this agreement expires on November 1, 2025.

GAP	GAP CLOSED
The defendant, in addition to having to pay punitive damages, may be liable for the plaintiff's costs and attorney fees.	The defendant may have to pay the plaintiff's costs and attorney fees in addition to punitive damages.

The problem is the same when the gap comes between the verb and the object:

> The proposed statute gives to any person who suffers financial injury by reason of discrimination based on race, religion, sex, or physical disability a cause of action for treble damages.

Here, a 21-word gap comes between the verb (gives) and the direct object (cause of action).

One remedy is to make two sentences. Another is to move the intervening words to the end of the sentence:

> The proposed statute gives a cause of action for treble damages to any person who suffers financial injury because of discrimination based on race, religion, sex, or physical disability.

➤ Exercise 10

Revise these sentences, putting the subject, verb, and object(s) close together and near the front of the sentence, and omitting as many surplus words as you can. Then look at the exercise key in the Appendix.

1. When, after an injury or harm allegedly caused by an event, measures are taken that, if taken previously, would have made the injury or harm less likely to occur, evidence of the subsequent measures is not admissible to prove negligence or other culpable conduct.

2. It is required by the law in virtually every jurisdiction that follows the common law that every witness shall, before giving

any testimony in the cause, declare that the testimony the witness shall give will be truthful, by an oath or affirmation in such form and content as is calculated to cause an awakening of the witness's conscience and impress the witness's mind with the duty to do so.

3. A lawyer, having offered her client's testimony in the belief that it was true, and having subsequently come to know that the evidence is false, must take "reasonable remedial measures," which includes as a first step remonstrating with the client in confidence, telling the client about the lawyer's duty of candor to the tribunal, and seeking the client's cooperation with respect to the withdrawal or correction of the false testimony.

4. The second remedial step, according to the *Restatement (Third) of the Law Governing Lawyers* § 120 (2000) and American Bar Association Model Code of Professional Responsibility, Rule 3.3, is for the lawyer, always seeking to cause the minimum amount of harm to the client and the client's legitimate objectives, to consider withdrawing from the representation, if withdrawal will undo the effects of the false evidence.

5. Disclosure of the falsehood to the tribunal, which is the third and ultimate remedial step and which is to be taken only after it becomes apparent that the first two steps are unavailing, is a drastic step in that the lawyer is allowed, in situations where it is necessary, to reveal information to the tribunal that would otherwise be protected by the attorney-client privilege and/or the ethical duty of confidentiality.

Put Conditions and Exceptions Where They Are Clear and Easy to Read

When lawyers draft contracts, statutes, rules, and the like, they often use conditions (if A and B, then C) and exceptions (D, except when E or F). One can imagine a language with strict rules about where in a sentence to put conditions and exceptions—for example, a rule that conditions always go at the beginning of the sentence and exceptions always go at the end. The English language has no such rules, so you must decide, sentence by sentence, where to put conditions and exceptions, guided by the need for clarity and readability.[1] Usually, the *end* of the sentence is the best place for a condition or exception, especially one that is longer than the main clause. For example:

> A lawyer may disclose a client's confidential information *if disclosure is necessary to prevent, mitigate, or rectify substantial injury to the financial interests or property of another that is reasonably certain to result or has resulted from the client's commission of a crime or fraud in furtherance of which the client has used the lawyer's services.*

Conversely, the *beginning* of the sentence is usually the best place if the condition or exception is short or needs to be at the beginning to avoid leading the reader astray. For example:

> *Except for U.S. citizens,* all persons passing this point must have in their possession a valid passport, a baggage clearance certificate, and a yellow entry card.

When you need to present multiple conditions or exceptions consider using an if-then table, as explained in Chapter 10.

When Necessary, Make a List

Sometimes the best way to present a cluster of closely related ideas is with an introductory clause followed by a list.[2] Here is a sentence that needs the list trick:

> You can qualify for benefits under Section 43 if you are 64 or older and unable to work, and that section also provides benefits in the event that you are blind in one eye, or both eyes, or are permanently disabled in the course of your employment.

The list trick transforms the sentence to this:

You qualify for benefits under Section 43 if you meet any one of the following conditions:

1. you are 64 or older and are unable to work; or
2. you are blind in one or both eyes; or
3. you are permanently disabled in the course of your employment.

When you use the list trick, begin with an introductory clause that tells the reader the purpose of the list. Then, follow these conventions:

- Make the items in the list parallel in substance. All items must relate to the same subject. In the list above, each item describes what makes someone eligible for benefits. Don't make a list like this:

  a. bread;

  b. eggs; and

  c. Nelson Mandela.

- Make the items in the list parallel in grammar. All items must have the same structure (noun, noun-verb, etc.). If the items have verbs, the verbs must all be in the same tense. In the list above about eligibility for benefits, each item has the same noun-verb structure, and the verbs are all in the same tense: *you are*. Don't make a list like this:

  a. jurisdiction;

  b. venue; and

  c. preparing charts for Dr. Sullivan's testimony.

- Connect items with *and* or *or* if necessary to make the relationships among the items clear to the reader. If the list is conjunctive, use *and* to separate items. If it is disjunctive, use *or*. The list above about eligibility for benefits is disjunctive because a person only needs to satisfy one of the listed criteria. Thus, the items are connected with *or*. If a person had to satisfy all of the criteria to be eligible, the items would have been connected with *and*. If both the list and the items are short, and if the reader will not become confused, you can use *and* or *or* only to separate the last two items. Also, you don't need *and* or *or* if the list is neither conjunctive nor disjunctive.

- **Use numbers or letters for lists of sequential items.** If the order of the items matters, a numbered or lettered list makes the sequence apparent to the reader. If the order does not matter, you can use bullets, numbers, or letters. For example, you should number the items in a list of instructions that must be followed in order.[3]

- **Use appropriate punctuation.** This list, for example, is a series of complete sentences, so each item begins with a capital letter and ends with a period. The list above about eligibility for benefits contains items that are not complete sentences, so it is punctuated differently. For a list like that, begin each item with a lower-case letter and separate items with semicolons. After the last item, end the list with a period.[4]

- **Make a list within a list if necessary.** In a complicated drafting task, you may find that an item in a list is complex enough to require a sub-list of its own. You can create a list within a list, but try not to use more than two ranks of lists. A list within a list within a list will be too hard for a reader to follow.

Although the list trick can help you present complex material effectively, your document should not read like a slide show presentation. Integrate lists to complement your text, not as a substitute for complete sentences and paragraphs.

> ## Exercise 11

Revise the following passages. Omit surplus words, put conditions and exceptions where they are clear, and use the list trick where appropriate. Then look at the exercise key in the Appendix.

1. The advance health care directive permits medical treatment to be discontinued if an individual has an incurable and irreversible condition that will result in the cessation of all bodily functions within a relatively short time, or becomes unconscious and, to a reasonable degree of medical certainty, will not regain consciousness, or the likely risks and burdens of treatment outweigh the expected benefits.

2. A health care provider, unless an advance directive giving contrary instructions is signed by the patient, will not withhold or withdraw treatment from a patient.

3. A provider of health care, which means a nurse or doctor, as well as a physician's assistant, nurse practitioner, and emergency medical technician, is required to comply with the patient's instructions regarding continuation of treatment.

4. Provided that it does not exceed the limitations imposed by its charter, or by the laws of the sovereign State of South Carolina, or by the laws of the United States of America, or by the Constitution of the United States of America, or by the Constitution of the sovereign State of South Carolina, a homeowners' association chartered by the sovereign State of South Carolina has the implied power to make reasonable rules concerning use of the common property of the association's members.

Put Modifying Words Close to What They Modify

In some languages, the order of words within a sentence does not affect the meaning of the sentence. But in English, word order does affect meaning. Modifying words tend to do their work on whatever you put them near. Putting a modifier in the wrong place can alter the meaning of your sentence or make its meaning unclear. Therefore, as a general rule, put modifying words as close as you can to the words you want them to modify.

Separating a modifier from the word it modifies leads to sentences like this:

> My client has discussed the proposal to fill the drainage ditch with his partners.

Is the proposal really to fill a drainage ditch with the client's partners?

Introductory clauses in particular are traps for the unwary. When you use an introductory clause that modifies a noun in the sentence, take care that it modifies the right noun. Otherwise, you will end up with sentences like these:

> Being unfit to stand trial, Judge Weldon ordered the petitioner's transfer to a state psychiatric hospital.

> Having been deployed overseas by the Navy, the prosecutor acknowledged that the witness was unavailable to testify.

Is Judge Weldon unfit to stand trial? Was the prosecutor deployed overseas?

Writers are prone to fall into this trap when they use introductory clauses to vary their sentence length and structure. You can use introductory clauses effectively as long as you keep modifying clauses close to the words they modify. One option for solving a separation problem is making the noun being modified the subject of the introductory clause:

> Because *the petitioner* was unfit to stand trial, Judge Weldon ordered him transferred to a state psychiatric hospital.

Another option is making the noun being modified the subject of the sentence:

Having been deployed overseas by the Navy, *the witness* was unavailable to testify, as the prosecutor acknowledged.

Modifier placement can also cloud meaning. One perpetrator of ambiguity is the "squinting modifier" — one that sits mid-sentence and can be read to modify either what precedes it or what follows it:

A trustee who steals dividends often cannot be punished.

What does *often* modify? Does the sentence tell us that crime frequently pays? Or that frequent crime pays?

Once discovered, a squinting modifier is easy to cure. Either choose a word that does not squint or rearrange the sentence to avoid the ambiguity:

Often a trustee who steals dividends cannot be punished.

The word *only* is a notorious troublemaker. For example, in the following sentence the word *only* could go in any of seven places (marked with asterisks) and produce a half a dozen different meanings:

* She * said * that * he * shot * her *.

To keep *only* under control, put it immediately before the word you want it to modify. If it creates ambiguity in that position, try to isolate it at the beginning or end of the sentence:

AMBIGUOUS	CLEAR
Lessee shall use the vessel only for recreation.	Lessee must use the vessel for recreation only.
Shares are sold to the public only by the parent corporation.	Only the parent corporation sells shares to the public.

Like a squinting modifier, a phrase that starts with a relative pronoun (like *who*, *which*, or *that*) can create ambiguity when the noun it modifies is unclear. Watch out for ambiguity in sentences like this one:

The grantor was Maxwell Aaron, the father of Sarah Aaron, who later married Pat Snyder.

Who married Pat — Maxwell or Sarah?

Some lawyers try to clear up this kind of ambiguity by piling on more words:

The grantor was Maxwell Aaron, father of Sarah Aaron, and said Maxwell Aaron later married Pat Snyder.

But it's easier than that. You can usually avoid ambiguity by placing the relative pronoun immediately after the word to which it relates. If Pat's spouse were Maxwell, the sentence could be rearranged to read:

The grantor was Sarah Aaron's father, Maxwell Aaron, who later married Pat Snyder.

Sometimes a relative pronoun will not behave, no matter where you put it:

Claims for expenses, which must not exceed $100, must be made within 30 days.

What must not exceed $100 — the claims or the expenses? Here the best remedy is simply to omit the relative pronoun:

Claims for expenses must not exceed $100 and must be made within 30 days.

or

Expenses must not exceed $100. Claims for expenses must be made within 30 days.

➢ Exercise 12

Revise these sentences to solve the modifier problems. If a sentence has more than one possible meaning, select whichever one you wish and revise the sentence to express that meaning unambiguously. Then look at the exercise key in the Appendix.

1. The builder only said that the smoke detectors complied with the new building code.

2. The court's opinion ignores the changes to the privacy policy adopted after the data breach.

3. After being subjected to retaliation by his supervisor, counsel argued that the plaintiff was constructively discharged.

4. Finding that she was a flight risk, the judge refused to release the defendant on bail.

5. The new dairy regulations were intended to reduce the open-air discharge of methane gas by the Department of Agriculture.

Avoid Noun Chains

Be careful when you use a series of nouns as adjectives modifying another noun. The result is a noun chain that is likely to strangle the reader. Technical writers like noun chains because they condense complex ideas into a single phrase, such as *draft laboratory animal rights protection regulations* and *public service research dissemination program proposals*. Readers, on the other hand, have trouble following noun chains.

To bring a noun chain under control, lop off any of the nonessential descriptive words. If that is not enough, move some words into prepositional phrases to break up the chain, like this: "*draft regulations to protect the rights of laboratory animals.*"

Avoid Nested Modifiers

You are likely familiar with Russian nesting dolls. They are hollow wooden dolls that separate in the middle. Separating the doll reveals a smaller doll inside. The second doll likewise comes apart to reveal a third, and the third a fourth.

Lawyers are prone to write sentences that are constructed like Russian nesting dolls. For example:

The defendant, who was driving a flatbed truck that was laden with a tangle of old furniture some of which was not tied down securely, stopped without warning.

Here is the same sentence written with brackets and parentheses:

The defendant {who was driving a flatbed truck [that was laden with a tangle of old furniture (some of which was not tied down securely)]} stopped without warning.

That sentence is like a Russian nesting doll because it contains a set of modifying phrases, each nested inside the next. The sentence is hard to understand because the reader must mentally supply brackets and parentheses to keep the modifiers straight.

The best remedy for such a sentence is to take apart the nest of modifiers and put some of the information in a separate sentence. Here is one possible revision:

The defendant was driving a flatbed truck that was laden with a tangle of old furniture, some of which was not tied down securely. She stopped without warning.

➤ Exercise 13

Revise these sentences. Omit surplus words, break up noun chains, and untangle nested modifiers. Then look at the exercise key in the Appendix.

1. Conflicts of interest, which can seriously erode, if not destroy entirely, the relationship of trust between attorney and client, are generally imputed to all attorneys in the firm.

2. One type of conflict of interest, in which an attorney enters into a business transaction of whatever kind, even a transaction that produces handsome profits for all concerned, with a client, can be solved if the attorney makes sure that adequate disclosures are made.

3. The terms of the transaction, which must be fair and reasonable to the client, must be disclosed, in a writing that uses clear, plain language, to the client.

4. Break up the following noun chains:
   a. multi-district litigation docket management procedures
   b. Commerce Clause preemption argument research
   c. coronary artery disease medication patent application
   d. client disbursement accounts restrictions

Clarify the Reach of Modifiers

Suppose that the owner of a pet store agrees to sell part of her stock to someone else. The contract of sale states that it covers "all female rabbits and hamsters over six-weeks-old." The contract is ambiguous, and the ambiguity is caused by the uncertain reach of the two modifiers *female* and *over six-weeks-old.* We can't tell whether *female* stops with *rabbits*, or whether it reaches forward to *hamsters* as well. Further, we can't tell whether *over six-weeks-old* stops with *hamsters*, or whether it reaches backward to *rabbits* as well. Thus, the contract may cover any of four combinations:

1. [all female rabbits, however old] + [all hamsters over six-weeks-old, of whatever sex]; or

2. [all female rabbits, however old] + [all female hamsters over six-weeks-old]; or

3. [all female rabbits over six-weeks-old] + [all hamsters over six-weeks-old, of whatever sex]; or

4. [all female rabbits over six-weeks-old] + [all female hamsters over six-weeks-old].

To avoid this kind of ambiguity, you must clarify the reach of the modifiers in your sentences. Sometimes you can do that simply by changing the word order:

AMBIGUOUS	CLEAR
women and men over 30	men over 30 and women
alto saxophones and bassoons	bassoons and alto saxophones

Other times, you can clarify the reach of a modifier by repeating words or making a list.

AMBIGUOUS	CLEAR
endangered frogs and salamanders	endangered frogs and endangered salamanders
all vans, sport utility vehicles, autos, and trucks without four-wheel drive	all vehicles without four-wheel drive, including vans, sport utility vehicles, autos, and trucks

Lest you think this type of ambiguity does not have serious consequences, take a look at *Lockhart v. United States*, 577 U.S. ___, 136 S. Ct. 958 (2016). The case turns on the reach of a modifying phrase in a federal sentencing statute. The statute imposes a mandatory minimum sentence for a federal offense when the defendant has previously been convicted "under the laws of any State relating to aggravated sexual abuse, sexual abuse, or abusive sexual conduct involving a minor or ward."

What is the reach of the modifying phrase *involving a minor or ward*? The mandatory minimum sentence unquestionably applies when a prior conviction relates to "abusive sexual conduct involving a minor or ward." But does the modifying phrase also reach the other two types of listed offenses?

The majority and dissent each invoked different principles of statutory interpretation to analyze the text. The majority ruled that the phrase has a short reach, modifying only the words that come immediately before it (abusive sexual conduct), and not the other two items in the list. Thus, *any* prior conviction relating to aggravated sexual abuse or sexual abuse, even if it does not involve a minor or ward, triggers the mandatory minimum sentence. The dissent concluded that the phrase has a long reach, modifying all the items in the list. In the dissent's analysis, a prior conviction relating to aggravated sexual abuse or sexual abuse would have to involve a minor or ward to trigger the mandatory minimum sentence.

You don't have to memorize rules of statutory interpretation to avoid these types of ambiguities. Simply clarify the reach of your modifiers.

➤ Exercise 14

Clarify the reach of the modifiers in these sentences. If a sentence has more than one possible meaning, select whichever one you wish and revise the sentence to express that meaning unambiguously. Then look at the exercise key in the Appendix.

1. An attorney is allowed to reveal a client's confidential information to prevent death, serious bodily injury, or serious financial injury due to a crime the client is about to commit.

2. A witness's prior criminal conviction can be used for impeachment if it was a felony or misdemeanor involving dishonesty or false statement.

3. A corporation is liable for financial losses suffered by an investor due to the criminal conduct of a high-ranking officer or employee acting within the scope of his or her authority.

CHAPTER SEVEN

Choose Your Words Carefully

Here are two ways a lawyer might begin a letter to a client to explain why the lawyer's bill is higher than the client expected:

Example One

The statement for professional services that you will find enclosed herewith is, in all likelihood, somewhat in excess of your expectations. In the circumstances, I believe it is incumbent upon me to avail myself of this opportunity to provide you with an explanation of the causes therefor. It is my considered judgment that three factors are responsible for this development.

Example Two

The bill I am sending you with this letter is probably higher than you expected, and I would like to explain the three reasons why.

Example One is awful, is it not? It contains many of the faults we have already discussed — a flock of derivative nouns, for example. But notice also the choice of words in Example One. Why does its author say *statement for professional services* instead of *bill*? The client calls it a bill. So does the lawyer, usually. By tradition, the bill itself can be captioned *statement for professional services*. But this is supposed to be a friendly, candid letter to a client; let us call a bill a *bill*.

Why does the author of Example One use lawyerisms like *here-with* and *therefor*? To make the letter sound important? Why does the author use airy, abstract words like *circumstances, factors,* and *development*? Do they somehow add dignity? Finally, why does the author use ponderous phrases instead of the simple words used in Example Two?

EXAMPLE ONE	EXAMPLE TWO
in all likelihood	Probably
in excess of your expectations	higher than you expected
explanation of the causes	explain why

Of course, you should use terms of art when they are appropriate. But don't confuse using fancy-sounding words with writing "like a lawyer." Everyday language will serve you best most of the time. This Chapter explains word choices that will improve your writing. Use concrete, familiar, gender-neutral words. Use strong nouns and verbs to persuade. Avoid empty lawyerisms, multiple negatives, and distracting words and syntax.

Use Concrete Words

Abstractions make writing boring and sometimes hard to understand. To grip and move your reader's mind, use concrete words, not abstractions.

You can see the impact concrete words have by comparing two descriptions of the same event. Here is how Exodus 7:20–21 describes Moses inflicting a plague on Egypt:

He lifted up the rod and smote the waters of the river . . . and all the waters that were in the river were turned to blood. And the fish that were in the river died; and the river stank, and the Egyptians could not drink the water of the river; and there was blood throughout all the land of Egypt.

Here is a description of that same event using abstract words like those you might see in a technical report:

His rod came into contact with the water, resulting in significant pollution. The resultant toxification rendered the water unsuitable to sustain the indigenous population of aquatic vertebrates, caused olfactory discomfort, and reduced potability. Social, economic, and political disorientation were experienced to an unprecedented degree.

Which version paints a vivid picture in your mind?

The lure of abstract words is strong for lawyers. Expressing complex ideas in concrete terms can be difficult. Further, lawyers want to be cautious and to cover every possibility, while leaving room to wiggle out if necessary. The vagueness of abstract words therefore seems attractive. Particularly attractive are words like *basis, situation, consideration, facet, character, factor, degree, aspect,* and *circumstances:*[1]

In our present circumstances, the budgetary aspect is a factor which must be taken into consideration to a greater degree.

Perhaps that means "now we must think more about money," but the meaning is a shadow in the fog of abstract words.

Using abstract words also removes people and their actions from your writing, giving it an air of cosmic detachment. Every legal problem involves people and actions. Without people acting in the world, no legal problems would exist. Yet legal writing too often favors disembodied abstractions instead. Here is an example from federal copyright law:

Copyright protection subsists, in accordance with this title, in original works of authorship fixed in any tangible medium of expression, now known or later developed, from which they can be perceived, reproduced, or otherwise communicated, either directly or with the aid of a machine or device.[2]

Can you find any people in that sentence? Its focus is on original works of authorship, which presumably must be created by someone. But that someone is nowhere to be found in the sentence.

Unnecessary abstraction diverts attention from the actor and the action. Sometimes abstract language is necessary or useful. But unless you have a reason to be abstract, use concrete words instead.

When you find yourself struggling to express a complex legal idea, remember to ask yourself the key question you learned in Chapter 2: Who is doing what to whom? Bring those living creatures into your writing; make them move around and do things to each other. Suddenly abstraction will evaporate, and your writing will come alive. If you cannot figure out who is doing what to whom, you may not understand what you're trying to say.

Do not mistake abstraction of the sort you see in the examples above for the intentional, artful vagueness sometimes required in legal writing. For example, advocates sometimes strategically choose abstract words to describe unfavorable facts precisely to avoid creating a vivid picture in the reader's mind. If you represent the aggressor in a bar fight, you might describe the results of the fight as *facial contusions and abrasions*. If you represent the victim, you would use more concrete language: *a split lip, a bloody nose, and a black eye*.

Similarly, good legal writing sometimes contains intentionally abstract phrases to provide a general compass heading when mapping the trail in detail is not possible, as in *reasonable restrictions* or *best efforts*. These abstractions can be useful when a writer wants to convey a general standard but cannot foresee every set of facts that may arise.

Abstraction is a virtue only if it is both necessary and intentional. Knowing when to be vague and when to be concrete is part of the art of lawyering.

Use Familiar Words

Aristotle put the case for familiar words this way: "Style to be good must be clear. . . . Speech which fails to convey a plain meaning will fail to do just what speech has to do. . . . Clearness is secured by using the words . . . that are current and ordinary."[3] Given a choice between a familiar word and one that will send your reader groping for the dictionary, use the familiar word. The reader's attention is a precious commodity, and you cannot afford to waste it by creating distractions.

Unlike many writers, attorneys usually know who their readers will be, and their choice of words can be tailored accordingly. A patent lawyer who is writing a brief to be filed in the United States Court of Appeals for the Federal Circuit can use legal terms that might be perplexing if used in a letter to the lawyer's inventor-client. Conversely, in writing to the inventor-client, the patent lawyer can use scientific terms that would be hypertechnical if used in a legal brief. In either case, the needs of the reader must take precedence over the self-gratification of the writer.

Even among familiar words, prefer the simple to the stuffy. Don't say *termination* if *end* will do as well. Don't use *expedite* for hurry, or *elucidate* for explain, or *utilize* for use. But do not conclude that your vocabulary should shrink to preschool size. If an unfamiliar word is fresh and fits your need better than any other, use it — just don't *utilize* it.

Use Gender-Neutral Words

The very first section of the United States Code says that "words importing the masculine gender include the feminine as well."[4] That may be so in the statute books, but many readers will be distracted and offended if you use masculine terms to refer to people who are not necessarily male. On the other hand, many readers will be distracted by clumsy efforts to avoid gendered terms. Gender fluidity also affects word choices. Our society's views on the nuances of gender and gender identity continue to evolve, and some people do not identify as either male or female.

For all of these reasons, do not use gendered terms unnecessarily. Use gender-neutral words instead. Here are four ways to incorporate gender-neutral words in your writing:

First, don't use expressions that imply value judgments based on gender. (For example, *a manly effort*, or *a member of the gentle sex*.)

Second, use nongendered terms if you can do so without artificiality. For example, use *workers* instead of *workmen*, *reasonable person* instead of *reasonable man*, *flight attendant* instead of *stewardess*, and *staffed* instead of *manned*. If the nongendered version of a term sounds artificial (*waitperson, chairperson, mailperson*), use a different term (*server, chair, letter carrier*).

Third, use parallel construction when you are referring to people of two genders. (For example, *husbands and wives*, not *men and their wives*, or *President and Mr. Watson*, not *President Watson and Harold*.)

Fourth, don't use a gendered pronoun when referring generally to people who may not be of that gender. For instance, don't use *he* every time you refer to judges. You can resort to the phrase *he or she* in moderation, but the better practice is to avoid gendered words altogether by using one of the following devices:

THIS DEVICE	CHANGES GENDERED PHRASING	TO GENDER-NEUTRAL PHRASING
Omit the pronoun.	*the average citizen enjoys his time on the jury*	*the average citizen enjoys jury duty*
Use second person instead of third person.	*each juror must think for herself*	*as a juror, you must think for yourself*
Use plural instead of singular.	*each juror believes that he has done something worthwhile*	*all jurors believe that they have done something worthwhile*

THIS DEVICE	CHANGES GENDERED PHRASING	TO GENDER-NEUTRAL PHRASING
Repeat the noun instead of using a pronoun.	*a juror's vote should reflect her own opinion*	*a juror's vote should reflect that juror's own opinion*
Use the passive voice. (For the reasons explained in Chapter 4, use this device only if no other option works.)	*a juror must submit an application to the court to defer his jury service*	*an application to defer jury service must be submitted to the court*

When using pronouns to refer to a particular individual, use the pronouns that person uses. Refer to a transgender person with pronouns that align with the person's gender identity. Ordinarily, you should use a singular pronoun to refer to a specific individual, as in "The juror stated her view of the evidence." A person who identifies as nonbinary, however, may use the plural pronouns *they* and *them* instead of gendered singular pronouns, as in "The juror stated their view of the evidence." As discussed more fully below, the singular *they* does not enjoy universal acceptance, but you should use it if that is the pronoun an individual prefers.[5]

Use Strong Nouns and Verbs to Persuade

Some legal writing is declaratory. It states facts and obligations without taking a position. Statutes, apartment leases, corporate by-laws, and bills of lading fall in this category. But some legal writing seeks to persuade the reader to believe what the writer believes. Legal briefs and judicial opinions are obvious examples. When you seek to persuade, you may choose to characterize facts in ways that favor your position. Your persuasive writing will be more potent if you use strong nouns and verbs to characterize, not weak nouns and verbs held afloat by adjectives and adverbs. For instance:

ADJECTIVE AND ADVERBS	NOUNS AND VERBS
The witness intentionally testified untruthfully about the cargo.	The witness lied about the cargo.
The defendant's sales agents maliciously took advantage of people with scant resources.	The defendant's sales agents preyed on the poor.

Deciding when to use characterizations can be tricky. Characterizations portray facts in ways that your reader may question. Once you decide to use a characterization, however, choose one that fits. Do not try to blunt its impact with weak words. To testify untruthfully is to lie. If that is what you mean to say, say it.

Similarly, do not use a fiery word and then douse it with water:

rather catastrophic

somewhat terrified

a bit malevolently

Likewise, do not choose a flaccid word and then try to prop it up with words like *very* and *quite*:

WEAK	STRONG
she was very, very angry	she was enraged
this is quite puzzling	this is baffling

➢ Exercise 15

Revise the passages below according to the instructions provided with each item. Then look at the exercise key in the Appendix.

1. Revise this passage, omitting surplus words and using concrete, familiar words whenever possible:

    Effectuation of improvement in the efficiency of the micro-lending market in the nations of Central America is dependent in part upon the creation of innovative methods of sharing loan default data among lenders without incentivizing mutual engagement in non-competitive collaboration on interest rates and risk assessment.

2. Revise this passage. Omit surplus words, use concrete, familiar words whenever possible, and address the passage directly to the reader:

    Property belonging to a client and coming into a lawyer's possession in connection with a representation must be kept separate from the lawyer's own property. In the case of client's funds coming into the lawyer's possession, they must be deposited in a separate account that has the incidents of a fiduciary account, which account must be maintained in the state in which the lawyer maintains his or her offices, or in another state but only with the consent of the client. In the case of a client's property other than funds coming into the lawyer's possession, it shall be identified as such and maintained in a place of safety consistent with its size and nature.

3. Revise this passage using appropriately strong nouns and verbs rather than adjectives and adverbs:

    The defendant corporation engaged in a reprehensible campaign of untruthful advertising, the object of which was to mislead people who have almost no resources and whose life experience and rudimentary schooling provide them relatively little scientific knowledge. Defendant, for the selfish purpose of augmenting its own revenues, undertook a program of misinformation, hoping to cause these unfortunate people to believe that antiretroviral drugs are causally connected with impotence, and that the defendant's multi-vitamin pills are more beneficial than antiretroviral drugs in combating HIV.

4. Revise the following sentences, incorporating gender-neutral language and eliminating surplus words:

   a. Not only may a judge examine witnesses called by the parties, he may also call witnesses himself whom the parties might not have called.

   b. A prosecutor may sometimes inveigle a judge to call a hostile but essential witness whom the prosecutor herself needs but fears to call. When a judge calls such a witness, she can question them from the bench, which often diminishes their hostility and makes them a more useful witness.

   c. Because a patient may claim that her treatment fell below the standard of medical care, a doctor must maintain his insurance policy in relation to malpractice claims.

Avoid Empty Lawyerisms

Lawyerisms are words like *aforementioned, whereas,* and *hereinafter.* They give writing a legal smell, but they carry little or no legal substance. When they are used in writing addressed to nonlawyers, they confuse and annoy. When used in other legal writing, they give a false sense of precision.

A lawyer's words should not differ without reason from the words used in ordinary English. Sometimes there is a reason. For example, the Latin phrase *res ipsa loquitur* has become a term of art that lawyers use to communicate among themselves, conveniently and with a fair degree of precision, about a tort law doctrine. But too often lawyers use Latin or archaic English phrases needlessly. Sometimes they do it out of habit or haste; the old phrase is the one they learned in law school, and they have never taken time to question its use. Other times they do it believing mistakenly that the old phrase's meaning cannot be expressed in ordinary English or that the old phrase is somehow more precise than ordinary English.

Consider, for example, the word *said* in its archaic use as an adjective. No lawyer in dinner-table conversation says: "The green beans are excellent; please pass said green beans." Yet legal pleadings come out like this:

> The object of said conspiracy among said defendants was to fix said retail prices of said products in interstate commerce.

Lawyers who use *said* claim that it is more precise than ordinary words like *the,* or *this,* or *those.* They say it means "the exact same one mentioned above." But the extra precision is either illusory or unnecessary, as the above example shows. If only one conspiracy has been mentioned in the preceding material, we will not mistake *this* conspiracy for some other conspiracy. *Said* is unnecessary. If more than one conspiracy has been previously mentioned, *said* does not tell us which of the several is meant. The extra precision is thus illusory. If *the* were put in place of all the *saids,* the sentence would be no less precise and much less clumsy.

Aforementioned is *said's* big brother, and it is just as useless. "The fifty-acre plot aforementioned shall be divided. . . ." If only one fifty-acre plot has been mentioned before, *aforementioned* is unnecessary, and if more than one fifty-acre plot has been mentioned before, then *aforementioned* is imprecise. When precision is important, use a specific reference: "The fifty-acre plot described in paragraph 2(f) shall be divided. . . ."

The moral is this: do not be too impressed by the Latin and archaic English words you read in law books. Their antiquity does not make them superior. When you are tempted to use a lawyerism, stop to see if your meaning can be expressed as well or better in a word or two of ordinary English.

Avoid Multiple Negatives

Beware of sentences that contain more than one negative expression. "It is unlawful to fail to . . ." is an example of a double negative. The grammar is proper, but the construction is hard to follow — it makes the reader's mind flip from *yes* to *no* to *yes*.

In addition to ordinary negative words and prefixes (such as *not*, *un-*, and *non-*), many other words operate negatively (for example, *terminate, void, denial, except, unless*, and *other than*). If you string a few of these negative words together, you can make the reader's eyes cross, like this:

> Provided, *however*, that this license shall *not* become *void unless* licensee's *failure* to provide such notice is *unreasonable* in the circumstances.

When you find that you have written a sentence with multiple negatives, identify each negative term. Then pair as many of them as you can to turn them into positives. Finally, rewrite the sentence using as many positives and as few negatives as you can. For instance, "it is unlawful to fail to stop at a red light" becomes "a driver must stop at a red light."

Here is a more complicated passage:

> No rate agreement shall qualify under Section 2(a) unless not fewer than thirty days' notice is given to all customers; and unless said rate agreement has been published, as provided above, provided however, that the publication requirement shall not apply to emergency rates; and until said rate agreement has been approved by the Commission.

The list trick described in Chapter 6 can help you rewrite this kind of complex passage using positives. The example above emerges like this:

> To qualify under Section 2(a), a rate agreement must meet these three conditions:

1. all customers must receive at least thirty days' notice of the rate agreement; and
2. the rate agreement must be published as provided above, unless it involves emergency rates; and
3. the rate agreement must be approved by the Commission.

Avoid Distracting Words and Syntax

Word choices and syntax that distract readers draw their minds from *what* you are saying to *how* you are saying it. Most people read legal writing, not because they want to, but because they have to. Their attention is therefore prone to wander. Further, they are usually surrounded by outside distractions — the ping of an email notification, the ring of the phone, and the clock that tells them time is short. Certain choices add to those distractions and thus should be avoided. These include:

- employing elegant variation;
- using they to refer to courts and other singular entities;
- splitting an infinitive; and
- ending a sentence with a preposition.

Elegant variation means using different words to refer to the same thing. Writers who employ elegant variation had English teachers who told them not to use the same word twice in proximity. Elegant variation produces sentences like this:

The first case was settled for $200,000, and the second piece of litigation was disposed of out of court for $300,000, while the price of the amicable accord reached in the third suit was $500,000.

Readers are left to ponder the difference between a *case, a piece of litigation,* and a *suit.* By the time they conclude that there is no difference, they have no patience left for *settled, disposed of out of court,* and *amicable accord,* much less for what the writer was trying to tell them in the first place.

Elegant variation is particularly vexing in technical legal writing. The reader of a legal document is entitled to assume that a shift in terms is intended to signal a shift in meaning and will be justifiably puzzled by passages like this:

> The use fee shall be 1% of Franchisee's gross revenue. Franchise payment shall be made on or before the 15th day of each month.

Are *franchise payments* something different from the *use fee*? If so, what are they, and when must the use fee be paid?

The problem is compounded in electronic documents. Readers are accustomed to using the search function to locate specific terms or passages. Elegant variation stymies their efforts to navigate the document.

Do not be afraid to repeat a word if it is the right word. Repeating it will avoid confusion and make your document more useful to the reader.

The singular *they* is another distractor. Traditionally, *they* could not properly refer to a singular noun like *court*. Habit and necessity are causing this to change. We use the singular *they* colloquially. It is accepted in news reporting[6] and, as noted above, is necessary to refer to some people properly. But many readers find the singular *they* off-putting. To avoid this reaction, limit use of the singular *they* to people who use it to refer to themselves. Use *it* to refer to a court, corporation, agency, or other singular entity.

Two additional distractions are splitting an infinitive and ending a sentence with a preposition. Many people have been taught not to split an infinitive. An infinitive is split when a modifier is inserted between the word *to* and the verb, for example, "to not split." This rule has been debunked by experts.[7] Nevertheless, some readers will be distracted when they see an infinitive split unnecessarily. Therefore, do not split an infinitive unless doing so will avoid an ambiguity or a clumsy expression.[8] Likewise, do not end a sentence with a preposition unless you must. Although we frequently end sentences with prepositions, doing so evinces a more casual tone than is appropriate for most legal writing.[9]

➤ Exercise 16

Revise the passages below according to the instructions provided with each item. Then look at the exercise key in the Appendix.

1. Revise the passages that follow. Use familiar, concrete words and omit surplus words and empty lawyerisms:

    a. In *Simpson v. Union Oil Co.*, Justice William O. Douglas announced, *ipse dixit*: "The patent laws which give a seventeen-year monopoly on 'making, using, or selling the invention' are *in pari materia* with the antitrust laws and modify them *pro tanto*. That was the *ratio decidendi* of the *General Electric* case."

    b. Appearances then were duly entered, Cecilia Wickham, Esq., *pro querente,* and defendant Augustine Crowell *in propria persona.*

2. Revise the passages that follow, eliminating as many negative expressions as possible:

    a. We urge the court not to refuse to consider the objections to the denial of the motion to dismiss the complaint.

    b. It is our position that the oral statement in question is not made inadmissible by the rule against hearsay evidence.

3. Revise this passage, addressing it directly to the reader. Omit surplus words and eliminate the elegant variation:

    Lawyers who practice before the courts are subject to local court rules, which govern matters of efficient court administration, such as what size paper to use for documents to be filed in court. Litigators must also be mindful of the preferences of individual judges, such as whether counsel are to stand or sit when questioning a witness. But most important to the courtroom attorney are the litigation principles that have been enshrined as rules of legal ethics. The ethics canons say, for example, that an attorney must not take a frivolous legal position, that is to say one that the attorney knows cannot be supported by the present law or by a good faith argument for changing the law. Similarly counsel must not express a personal opinion about a fact in issue or the credibility of a witness, and counsel must not make arguments to the jury that have not been supported by evidence in the record.

4. Revise the sentences that follow, avoiding the singular they:

    a. The prosecution stated their objection to the motion to suppress.

    b. The court issued their opinion on the qualified immunity defense.

    c. The corporation failed to notify their shareholders about the inventory losses.

    d. Any driver involved in an accident must provide their insurance information.

5. Choose in the appropriate pronoun to complete the following sentence:

    The plaintiff described _____ injuries to the jury.

    a. The plaintiff identifies as a woman.

    b. The plaintiff identifies as a transgender man.

    c. The plaintiff identifies as nonbinary and uses nongendered pronouns.

Use Commas Carefully

Careful punctuation is essential to clear writing. Readers rely on punctuation to understand a writer's meaning. Careless or incorrect punctuation makes meaning unclear. Punctuating is not a task that can be delegated to proofreaders or assistants. You must master punctuation rules to say what you mean to say. Lawyers have a professional duty to express meaning as clearly as possible, and that includes punctuating carefully.[1]

This Chapter and the next are guides to proper punctuation. They conform to ordinary English usage. But on some points, style and usage guides disagree. On those points, we have suggested the approach that will produce clarity with as little complexity as possible. These Chapters will not answer *all* of your punctuation questions. For that, you may need to consult modern grammar, style, and citation texts.[2]

This Chapter focuses on proper use of commas. The next Chapter addresses other punctuation marks. We devote an entire Chapter to commas because commas (or the lack of them) cause more mischief in the law than all of the other punctuation marks combined. This Chapter first defines terms you need to know to understand punctuation. It then addresses comma usage.

Definitions of Terms

Punctuation is easier if you remember a few definitions:

SUBJECT: The word or group of words that a clause or sentence makes a statement about.

- The *lawyer* had objected to the evidence.

PREDICATE: The word or group of words that makes a statement about the subject. The complete predicate is the main verb plus any modifiers and complements attached to it.

- The lawyer *had objected to the evidence.*

The simple predicate is the main verb (with its helping verbs).

- The lawyer *had objected* to the evidence.

PHRASE: A group of closely related words that does not contain both a subject and a predicate.

- *The lawyer in the gray skirt . . .*
- *Objecting to the evidence . . .*

INDEPENDENT CLAUSE: A group of words that contains both a subject and a predicate and that grammatically could stand alone as a complete sentence.

- *The lawyer in the gray skirt objected to the evidence.*

DEPENDENT CLAUSE: A group of words that contains both a subject and a predicate, but that grammatically could not stand alone as a complete sentence.

- *When the lawyer in the gray skirt objected to the evidence . . .*

A dependent clause frequently begins with a subordinating word, such as *who, which, when, that, since,* or *because.* A dependent clause can function as an adjective, an adverb, or a noun.

- The lawyer *who wore the gray skirt* objected to the evidence. [adjective — describes lawyer]

- *When the lawyer in the gray skirt objected*, the judge sustained the objection. [adverb — tells when]
- The judge agreed *that the evidence was inadmissible.* [noun — tells what]

➤ Exercise 17

In the sentences below, identify the specified sentence components. Then look at the exercise key in the Appendix.

1. Identify the subject and simple predicate (i.e., verb) in the sentences that follow. If one of these elements is missing, revise the sentence to make it grammatically correct.

    a. From 1776 until the end of the War of 1812, the overriding question was whether the nation could survive.

    b. During those formative years, the weakest of the three branches of government being the judiciary.

    c. Not particularly brightening the outlook, the President's appointment of John Marshall to the Court in 1801, supported unenthusiastically even by the Federalists.

    d. Under John Marshall's guidance, the Court consolidated far-reaching judicial power and put Congress's authority on a broad and permanent constitutional footing.

2. Identify the dependent and independent clauses in each of the following sentences:

    a. The Jeffersonians were certain that the Constitution was a limiting document and that John Marshall was a malignant force.

    b. They charged the Chief Justice with usurping power, and they further charged him with converting his colleagues to his plans for aggrandizement.

    c. The Federalists, on the other hand, expected the Court to consolidate national power and contain the emerging forces of democracy.

Comma Usage

Use commas to:

- connect two independent clauses with a conjunction;
- set off an introductory element;
- set off nonessential elements from the rest of the sentence;
- separate items in a list; and
- set off dates, titles, geographical names, and short quotations.

Use a Comma to Connect Two Independent Clauses With a Conjunction

An independent clause can stand on its own as a complete sentence. When you use a coordinating conjunction (*and, but, or, for, nor, yet,* and *so*) to link two independent clauses into one sentence, you must put a comma before the conjunction. In our many years of teaching writing to law students, we have found this to be one of the most common punctuation errors.

	subject	simple predicate		coordinating conjuction
The	defendant intentionally	accessed	the government computer system,	*and*
	she intentionally	denied	access to authorized users.	

and

	subject		simple predicate	coordinating conjuction
The	worm	that the defendant inserted in the operating system	multiplied a million fold,	*yet*
the	defendant		claimed	that he did not intend to damage the system.

To join two independent clauses properly with a coordinating conjunction, you need both the comma and the conjunction. If you use only the comma without the conjunction, you will be guilty of a "comma splice," a grievous sin. If you use only the conjunction without the comma, you create a run-on sentence.

On the other hand, when you have one subject with two verbs joined by a conjunction, do not use a comma, as in this example:

| | simple | | coordinating |
| subject | predicate | | conjuction |

The <u>defendant</u> intentionally <u>accessed</u> the government computer system *and*

intentionally   <u>denied</u>   access to authorized users.

➤ Exercise 18

Revise the sentences below, correcting the comma usage as necessary or explaining why the sentence is correct as written. Then look at the answer key in the Appendix:

1. At least one precedent exists for nonjudicial action by allies against a former enemy leader whose acts seem abhorrent, that precedent is the case of Napoleon.

2. Napoleon escaped from exile in Elba, and he marched again on Europe.

3. Representatives of all the European states except France declared Napoleon beyond the law, and had to resolve the question of what to do about him.

4. The Prussians said to shoot him but the Russians advocated more delicately for summary execution.

Use a Comma After an Introductory Element

Ordinarily you should put a comma after an introductory element, such as a phrase or clause.

- Wanting to settle the case quickly, the plaintiff authorized her lawyer to accept any amount over $5,000.
- At the time of the accident, the defendant was intoxicated.
- To make the point clearly, she used a diagram.

Omit the comma, however, if the introductory element is very short.

- At home he wears glasses instead of contact lenses.

Additionally, omit the comma if the introductory element is followed by inverted word order.

- From the apartment above came a loud scream.

➢ Exercise 19

Review the sentences below, correcting the comma usage as necessary or explaining why the sentence is correct as written. Then look at the answer key in the Appendix:

1. After Napoleon escaped from Elba came renewed calls for his execution.
2. Having condemned the execution of Louis XVI the European leaders would have been embarrassed to execute Napoleon.
3. To punish Napoleon for his actions the leaders resolved to exile him to St. Helena.
4. Upon exile Napoleon was out of the way and kept at British expense.

Use Commas to Set Off Nonessential Elements from the Rest of the Sentence

Use commas to set off nonessential elements from the rest of the sentence. "Nonessential" in this context means not required for the sentence to retain its meaning. This is not to suggest that nonessential elements are meaningless. They are frequently useful because they add information or provide transitions to improve the flow of your writing. But if they are not necessary for the sentence to make sense, they should be set off with commas. More specifically, use commas to set off the following items:

- nonrestrictive clauses;
- parenthetical elements and terms of personal address; and
- transitional words.

NONRESTRICTIVE CLAUSES

A clause that is not essential to the meaning of a sentence is called a nonrestrictive element. A nonrestrictive element is set off with commas. An element that is essential to the meaning of a sentence is called a restrictive element. A restrictive element is not set off with commas. Stated differently, if removing an element from a sentence does not change meaning or create ambiguity, it is nonrestrictive and should be set off with commas.

You can see the difference in these two sentences:

- The car, which is blue, ran the red light.
- The car that ran the red light was blue.

The first sentence would still make sense even if you omitted *which is blue*. *Which is blue* is a nonrestrictive element, and it should be set off with commas. The second sentence, by contrast, needs the description of the car. Which car? The car *that ran the red light*. Those words are essential to the meaning of the sentence and form a restrictive element that is *not* set off with commas.

Below is a list of words you can use to help spot restrictive and nonrestrictive elements. The list is not complete or absolute, so use it only as a guide:

USUALLY NONRESTRICTIVE (SET OFF WITH COMMAS)	USUALLY RESTRICTIVE (NO COMMAS)	
which	that	while
although	because	if
though	before	when

Many words can introduce either restrictive or nonrestrictive elements. In those cases, you must evaluate the content to determine whether to set off the element with commas. Compare these examples:

- His father, who is an engineer, arrived on Tuesday.
- The employee who filed the complaint works in the Denver office.

An exception to this rule applies when a dependent clause comes at the beginning of a sentence. Always put a comma at the end of the dependent clause, even if it is essential to the meaning of the sentence.

- If you accept our conditions, we will postpone the hearing.

PARENTHETICAL ELEMENTS AND TERMS OF PERSONAL ADDRESS

When you insert a parenthetical element or term of personal address into a sentence, set off the interruption with commas.

A parenthetical element is inserted to explain or qualify the content of the sentence. It is pertinent but not essential to the meaning of the sentence and should be set off with commas.

- The mayor's indictment was, to say the least, unexpected.
- Freedom of speech is, after all, one of our most cherished rights.

Legal citations included in the text are parenthetical elements and should be set off by commas.

- In the *DeShaney* case, 489 U.S. at 192, the Court discussed that very point.

A term of direct address (*madam, sir, my friend,* and the like) can also be inserted into a sentence. When that happens, set off the interruption with commas.

- We submit, Your Honor, that the injunction should be lifted.

TRANSITIONAL WORDS

Use commas to set off transitional words (*therefore, thus, furthermore, moreover, as a result,* and the like) at the beginning or in the middle of a sentence.

- The conclusion, therefore, is that attorney advertising deserves only limited protection under the First Amendment.

If the transitional word separates two independent clauses, the rule is different. Using commas alone creates a comma splice. Instead, put a semicolon before the transitional word. Then, add a comma after it.

- Attorney advertising is a type of commercial speech; therefore, it deserves only limited protection under the First Amendment.

This is explained more fully with semicolons in Chapter 9.

➤ Exercise 20

Review the sentences below, revising them as necessary. Then look at the answer key in the Appendix:

1. Review the following sentences, correcting the comma usage as necessary or explaining why the sentence is correct as written.

   a. Lutz who sued Reliance Nissan for wrongful termination could not show that the arbitration clause in her employment contract was unconscionable.

   b. Conversely, the plaintiff who successfully challenged the arbitration clause produced evidence of unconscionability.

   c. The evidence of unconscionability which was overwhelming persuaded the court to decide the two cases differently.

   d. The opinion states among other things that unconscionable contracts are not enforceable.

   e. Lutz argued that she entered into the contract under duress, however the court was not persuaded.

   f. To explain its ruling therefore the court distinguished Lutz's case from the earlier case.

2. Review the sentences below, inserting *that* in any restrictive clauses and *which* in any nonrestrictive clauses.

   a. The defendant's motion, _____ asked the court to dismiss the complaint, was not served properly.

   b. The motion _____ the court granted was not dispositive.

   c. The corporation _____ employs the defendant may be vicariously liable for her actions.

   d. The plaintiff intends to rely on *res ipsa loquitur*, _____ is a tort law doctrine.

Use Commas to Separate Items in a Series

A SERIES OF CONNECTED ITEMS

When a sentence contains a series of three or more items joined with one conjunction, put commas after each item except the last.

- The defendant was armed with a sawed-off shotgun, a semi-automatic pistol, and a hunting knife when he entered the bank.

You may have been taught that the last comma (between *a semi-automatic pistol* and *a hunting knife*) is not necessary. The comma placed between the penultimate and last items in a series is sometimes called the Oxford comma. Respected modern sources differ about whether it is necessary. The sentence above would still be clear even without the Oxford comma, but that is not true for every sentence. Consider these examples:

- This book is dedicated to my parents, Ayn Rand and God.[3]
- The overtime rules do not apply to the canning, processing, marketing, storing, packing for shipment or distribution of agricultural products.

The first sentence is simply silly without the Oxford comma. The second cost a company five million dollars in overtime pay.[4] Is *packing for shipment or distribution* all one item or two separate items? If the phrase is all one item, the overtime rules do not apply to packing for distribution but do apply to other activities involved in distribution. If they are separate items, all activities involved in distribution, not just packing for distribution, are exempt from the overtime rules.

The lesson: In formal legal writing, use the Oxford comma to avoid ambiguity.

If the series is complicated or contains internal commas, use semicolons rather than commas between the items.

- The police search of the suspect's apartment produced engraving plates, which were of the type used for counterfeiting; a large quantity of ink, which apparently had been stolen from the government's ink supplier; and a variety of forged passports and other travel documents, which showed that the suspect had recently traveled to nine European countries.

A SERIES OF COORDINATE ADJECTIVES

When two or more adjectives are "coordinate," they modify a noun equally, and they should be separated with commas. Do not put a comma between the last adjective and the noun.

- The plaintiff was driving an <u>old</u>, <u>dusty</u>, <u>blue</u> *truck.*

Old, dusty, and blue all modify truck.

If the last adjective and the noun together form the term that is modified by the prior adjectives, do not use a comma before the last adjective.

- The plaintiff was driving an <u>old</u>, <u>dusty</u> *Ford truck.*

Here, old and dusty modify Ford truck.

If one adjective modifies another, do not separate them with a comma. To tell whether the adjectives are equal modifiers (and thus should be separated with commas), try mentally rearranging the adjectives or mentally inserting the word *and* between the adjectives. If the meaning does not change, the adjectives are equal modifiers (coordinates), and you should use a comma to separate them.

- A dark, cold night (*dark* and *cold* modify *night* equally).
- A bright red tie (*bright* modifies *red*; a "red, bright tie" states a different meaning).
- A strong constitutional argument (*strong* modifies *constitutional argument*).

➤ Exercise 21

Review the sentences below, correcting the comma usage as necessary or explaining why the sentence is correct as written. Then look
at the answer key in the Appendix:

1. Patents protect novel and nonobvious inventions, including
   medicines tools innovative processes and machines.

2. Patents encourage innovation by protecting novel nonobvious
   inventions.

3. Copyrights protect original works of authorship, such as
   books, including comic books and graphic novels, music, and
   artwork, including drawings and paintings.

4. Making an unauthorized copy of an original movie soundtrack
   is unlawful.

Use Commas to Set Off Dates, Titles,
Geographic Names, and Short Quotations

Respected modern sources differ about the use of commas in writing dates. These are commonly recommended formats:

- On April 8, 2024, a solar eclipse will be visible in North
  America.

- On 8 April 2024, a solar eclipse will be visible in North
  America.

Titles that follow a person's name are usually nonrestrictive and
should be set off with commas.

- Jane Sherwood, M.D., testified for the defense.

- Jacob Michaels, Esq., is the firm's newest partner.

Use commas to separate geographic place names (cities from
states, and states from nations).

- Seattle, Washington, is the defendant's principal place of
  business.

- Tokyo, Japan, is the plaintiff's principal place of business.

Use a comma to introduce a short quotation, unless it is incorporated into your sentence.

- The witness said, "The red car was speeding."
- The statute banned smoking "in any public building."

➤ Exercise 22

Review the sentences below, correcting the comma usage as necessary or explaining why the sentence is correct as written. Then look at the answer key in the Appendix:

1. The defendant began serving his sentence on November 10 2017 at the federal correctional facility in Anthony Texas.
2. The engineering report by Sandra Ellison Ph.D. concluded that, "the design was structurally sound."
3. The judge told the witness "Please answer the question."
4. The witness said she "saw the defendant clearly."

➤ Exercise 23

Review the sentences below. Using all the rules from this Chapter, correct the comma usage as necessary. Then look at the answer key in the Appendix:

1. On May 25 2018 Melissa Stanton sued Oak Valley Associates, the building contractor and the janitorial company.
2. Stanton alleges that she lives in Valdosta Georgia.
3. Heritage Corporation is the janitorial company, that serves Oak Valley Associates. Medical Facility Construction is the building contractor, and is owned by Arthur Marshall M.D.
4. The complaint which was filed exactly four years after Stanton was injured alleges ordinary negligence; gross negligence, and recklessness.

5. The defendants argue that the complaint was filed too late therefore they move to dismiss.

6. The three-year statute of limitations applies, defendants argue because the plaintiff's complaint seeks damages for personal injuries.

7. Stanton was in a long-term care facility for more than a year after the injury, and argues that the statute of limitations was tolled while she was incapacitated.

8. Because she was incapacitated Stanton was unable to pursue her claim.

9. The defendants however challenge that assertion.

10. Stanton's injuries include persistent tooth pain, which began immediately after her fall, jaw pain, which was exacerbated by a later injury in the long-term care facility, and headaches.

CHAPTER NINE

Use Other Punctuation Marks Carefully

This Chapter is a guide to punctuation marks other than commas. Like Chapter 8 on commas, this Chapter conforms to ordinary English usage as reflected in modern style and usage guides. Although this Chapter covers many aspects of punctuation, you may still need to refer to grammar, style, and citation texts to answer some punctuation questions.[1]

This Chapter explains how to use the following punctuation marks:

- periods, question marks, and exclamation points;
- semicolons;
- colons;
- parentheses;
- dashes;
- hyphens; and
- apostrophes.

For guidance on citation and quotation conventions in legal writing, you should consult a citation manual, such as the *ALWD Guide to Legal Citation* or the *Bluebook*.[2]

Periods, Question Marks, and Exclamation Points

USE PERIODS TO END SENTENCES OR
PUNCTUATE SOME ABBREVIATIONS

Use a period to end a declarative sentence, a command, or an indirect quotation.

- Serve the interrogatories today.

- She asked what day the interrogatory answers are due.

Follow common usage in putting periods in abbreviations. Some abbreviations use periods, and others do not. You can look up common abbreviations in a good dictionary, the *ALWD Guide to Legal Citation*, or the *Bluebook*. If you cannot find the abbreviation in those sources, you probably should not use it, unless your readers are sure to know what you are talking about. If an abbreviation with a period at the end comes at the close of a sentence, use only one period.

USE A QUESTION MARK TO END A DIRECT QUESTION

Put a question mark at the end of a direct question.

- To what extent is hate speech protected by the First Amendment?

- What would justify a writ of mandamus in this case?

Do not put a question mark at the end of an indirect question:

- The judge asked why our brief exceeded the page limit.

USE EXCLAMATION POINTS FOR EMPHASIS,
BUT ONLY RARELY

Exclamation points, which show surprise or strong emotion, are much like chili peppers. Used sparingly and in the right context, they add a piquant touch, but be careful. In formal legal writing, such as an appellate brief, exclamation points are almost never appropriate: they tend to be strident rather than persuasive. But in a client letter, email, or office memorandum, the occasional exclamation point will do no harm; if nothing else, it lets the writer blow off steam.

➤ Exercise 24

Review the sentences below, correcting the punctuation as necessary or explaining why the sentence is correct as written. Then look at the answer key in the Appendix:

1. The appellate judges asked why the trial court ruled the way it did.
2. Did the trial judge err by excluding the evidence.
3. Recovery for intentional infliction of emotional distress requires conduct that causes an average member of the community to exclaim, "Outrageous."

Semicolons

Some writers put semicolons and wild mushrooms in the same category: some are delicious, but others are deadly, and since it is hard to tell the difference, they should all be avoided. In truth, semicolons are not hard to master, and they can be very useful in two situations:

- to join two independent clauses; and
- to separate items in a complicated list.

Recall the definition of an independent clause from Chapter 8: A group of words that contains both a subject and a predicate and that grammatically could stand alone as a complete sentence, as in, "The lawyer in the gray skirt objected to the evidence." A more complete explanation of subjects, predicates, and clauses appears in Chapter 8. You should review that material if these terms are not familiar to you.

USE A SEMICOLON TO JOIN TWO INDEPENDENT CLAUSES WITHOUT A CONJUNCTION

As you learned in Chapter 8, one way to join two independent clauses is with comma followed by a coordinating conjunction like *and, or,* or *but.* Another way to join two independent clauses is with a semicolon. You can use a semicolon without a conjunction to join two closely related independent clauses; doing so adds variety to your writing and helps keep it from seeming choppy. Do not, however, join two independent clauses with a semicolon unless they are closely related. Here are two examples:

- The defense counsel objected to the question; she said that it called for information protected by the attorney-client privilege. (This is correct.)

- The plaintiff alleged that the defendant ran the stop sign; the court granted the motion to dismiss. (This is incorrect.)

USE A SEMICOLON TO JOIN TWO INDEPENDENT CLAUSES WITH A TRANSITIONAL EXPRESSION

Again, recall from Chapter 8 that a transition (such as *therefore, however, furthermore, thus, indeed, in fact, as a result,* or *for example*) at the beginning or in the middle of a sentence is set off with commas. When you use a transitional expression to join two independent clauses, however, commas alone will not do the job. Instead, put a semicolon before the transitional word or phrase. Then, add a comma after it.

These examples are correct:

- The court granted the preliminary injunction; therefore, the company could not fire the plaintiff while the case was pending.

- The witness had no personal knowledge of the event; in truth, her testimony was hearsay.

These examples are incorrect:

- The court granted the preliminary injunction, therefore, the company could not fire the plaintiff while the case was pending. (This is incorrect because *therefore* connects two independent clauses.)

- Once the court granted the preliminary injunction; therefore, the company could not fire the plaintiff while the case was pending. (This is incorrect because *therefore* connects a dependent clause with an independent clause.)

USE SEMICOLONS TO SEPARATE ITEMS IN A COMPLICATED SERIES

Ordinarily you should use commas to separate the items in a series, as explained in Chapter 8. But if the series is complicated or contains internal commas, use semicolons to separate the items.

- The prosecutor called the following witnesses: Susan Wu, a psychiatrist; Michael Bradford, a ballistics expert; and George Frye, a police investigator.

▷ Exercise 25

Review the sentences below, correcting the punctuation as necessary or explaining why the sentence is correct as written. Then look at the answer key in the Appendix:

1. Our economic system depends in part on legal recognition of property rights; and parties must be able to enforce their property rights when necessary.

2. Attorney conflicts of interest can arise in many settings, therefore, you must check for conflicts before accepting any new case.

3. The defendant is charged with horizonal price fixing, which is an antitrust offense, breach of contract in the sale of the business, and fraud, which is a common-law tort.

4. A motion to dismiss is filed before a responsive pleading; a motion for judgment on the pleadings is filed after the answer is filed.

Colons

A colon indicates that what follows is one of these:

- a series; or
- a summary, elaboration, or illustration of what precedes it; or
- a long quotation.

USE A COLON TO INTRODUCE A SERIES

When you use a colon to introduce a series, the material that precedes the colon must be able to stand alone as an independent clause. The independent clause can include *as follows* or *the following*, but it need not do so.

- We must subpoena the following witnesses: Barnes, Cruz, and Younger.
- We must subpoena three witnesses: Barnes, Cruz, and Younger.

Do not put a colon between a verb and its object or between a preposition and its object.

- We must subpoena: Barnes, Cruz, and Younger. (The colon is misused here because it separates the verb subpoena from its three objects.)
- We must serve a subpoena on: Barnes, Cruz, and Younger. (The colon is misused here because it separates the preposition on from its three objects.)

USE A COLON TO INTRODUCE A SUMMARY, ELABORATION, OR ILLUSTRATION

You can use a colon after an independent clause to introduce items that summarize, explain, or illustrate an idea addressed in the independent clause.

- The plaintiff failed to prove two key elements: negligence and proximate cause.

- The damages were staggering: $1,948,000 in medical bills and $74,000 in lost wages.

- Only one thing stands between us and settlement: money.

You can also use a colon to join two independent clauses if the first clause introduces the second.

- The DNA evidence is vital: it is our only proof that the defendant was at the scene.

USE A COLON TO INTRODUCE A LONG QUOTATION

You should ordinarily use a comma to introduce a short quotation, but if the quotation is longer than one sentence, use a colon.

- She invoked the words of Abraham Lincoln: "The Lord prefers common-looking people. That is the reason He makes so many of them."

➤ Exercise 26

Review the sentences below, correcting the punctuation as necessary or explaining why the sentence is correct as written. Then look at the answer key in the Appendix:

1. Rule 12 provides that the following defenses must be raised by motion before a responsive pleading; lack of subject-matter jurisdiction, lack of personal jurisdiction, and improper venue.

2. Judge Learned Hand was quoted as saying, "If we are to keep our democracy, there must be one commandment, thou shalt not ration justice."

3. As Eleanor Roosevelt said, "People grow through experience if they meet life honestly and courageously. This is how character is built."

Parentheses

USE PARENTHESES TO SET OFF INTERJECTED OR EXPLANATORY MATERIAL

Commas, parentheses, and dashes are all used to set off material that interrupts a sentence. The three differ in the emphasis they give to the material they set off. Commas tend to be neutral; they neither emphasize nor deemphasize the material. Parentheses deemphasize the material; they are used when the information is clearly subordinate. Dashes emphasize the material.

Here is an example of the kind of material that belongs in parentheses:

- The police found a diamond ring (worth at least $1,000) in the suspect's pants pocket.

The material inside the parentheses should be punctuated as necessary.

- In the suspect's pants pocket, the police found a diamond ring (worth at least $1,000) and three credit cards (MasterCard, Visa, and American Express).

USE PARENTHESES TO AVOID AMBIGUITIES

Used in moderation, parentheses can be helpful when you need to clarify what modifies what, or to interject a brief definition or qualification, or to state an exception.

- The levy established in subparagraph 9 does not apply to residential property (property used by a taxpayer as a primary residence).

- No deduction is allowed if the donor retains or transfers an interest (as defined above) in the property to any person other than the donee spouse (or the estate of the spouse).

USE PARENTHESES TO TABULATE ITEMS IN A SERIES

When a sentence lists several complex elements in a series, you can use numbers or letters enclosed in parentheses to indicate the intended divisions.

- The testator gave her sister-in-law three items: (a) 100 shares of Intel common stock, (b) the amethyst ring that had belonged to the testator's Aunt Dolores, and (c) an ancient calico cat, which had been the testator's constant companion.

USE PARENTHESES TO INTRODUCE ACRONYMS OR SHORTHAND REFERENCES

- The Eastern Region Trade Agreement (ERTA) prohibits any retaliatory tariff on agricultural commodities.

- Universal Communications, Inc. (UCI) developed the transverse uniflex modulator system ("the system") in 1994.

You do not need to use hereinafter in the parenthetical to indicate a shorthand reference unless your citation manual requires it for a proper citation.

➤ Exercise 27

Review the sentences below, correcting the punctuation as necessary or explaining why the sentence is correct as written. Then look at the answer key in the Appendix:

1. The proposed change to the tax law affects these groups: married filers who have been deducting state and local taxes

from their federal returns, both married and single filers who have been deducting interest on home equity loans, and single filers who have been claiming the earned income tax credit.

2. The Joint Committee on Taxation is charged with investigating the operation and effect of internal revenue taxes. The JCT a nonpartisan committee established by the Revenue Act of 1926 calculated the effects of the proposed change.

3. The proposed change will affect any taxpayer eligible to file as a head of household as set out in the statute.

Dashes

Dashes and hyphens look similar, but they are used for different purposes. A hyphen (-) is the short horizontal line that appears on your keyboard. Dashes are longer and come in two sizes. The longer dash is an em-dash (—). The shorter dash is an en-dash (–).

USE AN EM-DASH TO SIGNAL AN ABRUPT BREAK AND AN EN-DASH FOR A RANGE

An em-dash is the punctuation mark used to set off material that interrupts a sentence. As noted above, em-dashes emphasize the material:

- The judge — bristling with indignation — slammed the gavel on the bench.
- We need not reach the constitutional issue — that can await another day and another set of facts.

You should also use em-dashes instead of commas when you need to clearly set off material that needs to sit in the middle of a sentence because of what it modifies.[3]

- The magistrate may rule on any procedural motion — including a motion to suppress evidence and a motion to allow or disallow discovery — at any time following the acceptance of a plea.

The autocorrect settings in your word processing software may be set to convert two consecutive hyphens into an em-dash. If not, you should find the em-dash with other special characters. Do not include a space before or after an em-dash.

Use an en-dash (–) to indicate a range. It is used by itself, not with other words like *from* or *between*.[4]

- The summer semester runs from June 1–August 15.
  (This is incorrect.)
- The summer semester runs June 1–August 15.
  (This is correct.)
- The summer semester runs from June 1 to August 15.
  (This is also correct.)

As with an em-dash, do not include a space before or after an en-dash.

▷ Exercise 28

Review the sentences below, correcting the punctuation as necessary or explaining why the sentence is correct as written. Then look at the answer key in the Appendix:

1. Sewage sludge the substance at issue in this case differs from solid waste.
2. Farmers recognize the benefits-economic, ecological, and agricultural-of using disinfected sewage sludge for agricultural purposes.
3. The ideal time to use disinfected sewage sludge is during the May–July growing season.

Hyphens

USE UP-TO-DATE TERMINOLOGY

Some compound terms (terms that are formed from more than one word) are written as separate words (ice cream), some are hyphenated (brother-in-law), and some are written as a single word (textbook). Usage often changes over time. A compound term usually enters the language as two words (hard drive). As it becomes more familiar, it often grows a hyphen (binge-watch). When it becomes commonplace, it often becomes one word (handlebar). When you are in doubt, check the term in an up-to-date dictionary.

FOLLOW COMMON USAGE IN HYPHENATING COMPOUND MODIFIERS

If two or more words act together as a single modifier, they should usually be joined by a hyphen. Some of these compound modifiers are common and can be found in a dictionary (second-guess), but others are created to fit the need (nursing-home care). The following general principles, plus a large measure of your own common sense, will help avoid errors like the one in this sentence: "The new tax deduction is designed to aid small business owners." (Apparently the large ones must fend for themselves.)

Hyphenate only when the modifier precedes the term modified.

- My hard-headed boss
- My boss is hard headed.

Do not hyphenate if the first term is an adverb ending in -ly.

- An overly active imagination
- A radically different constitutional analysis

Do not hyphenate foreign phrases.

- A bona fide purchaser
- An ex post facto law

A hyphen is usually used with the prefixes ex-, self-, quasi-, and all-. A hyphen is usually not used after the prefixes anti, co, de, inter, intra, multi, non, para, pro, re, semi, or super — unless the second element is capitalized or the hyphen is needed to avoid confusion.

- Her ex-husband
- A self-inflicted wound
- The quasi-contract claim
- Antitrust law
- The anti-Communist forces
- Her paralegal assistant
- His redrafted brief

If two or more hyphenated compounds share a common element, you only need to use the shared element once:

- Long- and short-term budget reductions
- Pre- and post-judgment interest

USE HYPHENS FOR COMPOUND NUMBERS AND FRACTIONS

Use hyphens for numbers 21 through 99, even if they are part of a larger number.

- Thirty-eight
- One hundred thirty-eight

Use hyphens between all elements of a fraction.

- A one-third contingent fee
- A one-twenty-sixth share

▷ **Exercise 29**

Review the sentences below, correcting the punctuation as necessary or explaining why the sentence is correct as written. Then look at the answer key in the Appendix:

1. Sewage-sludge is a by-product of wastewater treatment that includes bio-solids. It is generally a solid or quasisolid, mud like substance, typically consisting of water and from 2%– 28% solids.

2. The state's environmental law categorizes any treated wastewater containing less than twenty eight percent solids as sewage sludge.

3. The judge did not wish to appear hard hearted in sentencing the defendant.

4. The public may criticize judges who are either especially-soft or hard hearted jurists.

Apostrophes

USE APOSTROPHES TO FORM POSSESSIVES

Modern authorities differ on how to form some possessives. Be aware that reasonable people can disagree passionately about the following rules.

To make the possessive of a singular noun, add 's, even if the word ends with an s sound. If that would make a triple s sound, then use an apostrophe only. For classical and biblical names that end in s, use an apostrophe only.

- Susan's running shoes
- Theodore James's new novel
- Defendant Jones's fingerprints
- Achilles' heel
- Zacharias' son, John the Baptist

To make the possessive of a plural noun that ends in an s sound, use an apostrophe only. If the plural ends in a different sound, use 's.

- The women's restroom
- The Joneses' house
- The clans' movement across the desert

If more than one owner is listed, you must decide whether the ownership is joint or individual. For joint ownership, form the possessive for the last owner listed. For individual ownership, form the possessive for each owner listed.

- Jesse's and Ula Mae's computers (each owns one)
- Bruce and Tim's sailboat (they own it together)

For compound expressions, form the possessive with the last element listed.

- The plaintiff was driving her mother-in-law's car.
- Your Honors' original order required payment of costs. (several judges entered the order)

Never put an apostrophe in a possessive pronoun (his, hers, its, yours, ours, theirs, whose). Remember that its is the possessive pronoun meaning "belonging to it." It's is a contraction for "it is" or "it has." You will always get this right if you remember that the apostrophe in it's takes the place of the missing letters in the verb. If you can't substitute it plus is or has for the contraction, you don't need the apostrophe.

Finally, if your ear tells you that a possessive sounds awkward, be bold and use a few glue words to form the possessive the long way. For example, "the index of the revised and expanded edition" is longer but sounds better than "the revised and expanded edition's index."

USE APOSTROPHES TO FORM CONTRACTIONS AND ABBREVIATIONS

In contractions and abbreviations, an apostrophe stands for the omitted letters. For example, can't, it's, wouldn't, Nat'l, and Ass'n. Remember that the contraction of have is 've, not the word of — would've for would have, not would of; should've for should have, not should of.

Because contractions convey informality, you should not use them in drafting statutes, court orders, contracts, appellate briefs, or other formal legal documents. They are, however, appropriate if you want a piece of legal writing to have a less formal tone. For example, some judges favor contractions in jury instructions because an informal tone is consistent with their personal style in delivering the instructions orally to the jury. Contractions are also appropriate if you want to set a less formal tone in a client letter, email, or office memorandum.

USE 'S TO FORM THE PLURAL OF SOME TERMS

In almost all cases, you will not use 's to form a plural. But of course, exceptions to this rule exist. Use 's to form the plural of abbreviations, numbers, letters, symbols, and words referred to as words. The modern trend is not to use an apostrophe in the plurals of years.

- Revise this contract by replacing all the aforementioned's with this's.
- The witness recalled that the license number included three 6's.
- She got mostly B's in law school.
- C.P.A.'s usually enjoy the tax courses.
- The Impressionists dominated the late 1800s.

➤ Exercise 30

Review the sentences below, correcting the punctuation as necessary or explaining why the sentence is correct as written. Then look at the answer key in the Appendix:

1. Good legal writing requires no hereinafter's or whereinbefore's.
2. Justice O'Connors' concurring opinion took issue with the majority's reliance on cases from the 1920s, before the expansion of Congress' power under the Commerce Clause. Her's is the more persuasive of the two opinion's.
3. A business' net worth is not always a good measure of its future profitability.
4. Alices and Teds fathers-in-law purchased the property together.

➤ Exercise 31

Review the sentences below. Using all the rules from this Chapter, correct the punctuation as necessary. Then look at the answer key in the Appendix:

1. The most common causes of attorney discipline are: alcohol and greed.
2. Defense counsel sat in silence, the evidence was admitted without objection.
3. The one-year statute of limitations has made our deadline's shorter. I don't like its effect because its created a hectic work environment.
4. We should listen to our instincts when assessing a legal arguments' validity.
5. Lay witnesses' can be paid for their expenses and time lost from work, however, a lay witness's request for additional payments cannot be granted.

6. Justice Ginsburg quoted Sarah Grimké, "I ask no favor for my sex. All I ask of our brethren is that they take their feet off our necks."

7. In a pre-mature appeal from the trial courts order, the plaintiff raises various meritless arguments.

8. The judge instructed counsel, "Call your next witness please?"

9. The Department of Labor DOL advises employers concerned about compliance to follow the safe harbor provisions Parts 1–3 of the regulations.

10. The plaintiffs attorney leaping to his feet shouted "Objection."

CHAPTER TEN

Use Easy-to-Read Design Techniques

The purpose of all writing is to convey meaning. The content of your writing is paramount in conveying meaning, and most of this book addresses ways to express content most effectively. But the way text looks cannot be divorced from the content. Design choices that discourage readers from reading or make understanding your content difficult undermine your purpose. Especially with electronic communications, the appearance of text affects meaning and comprehension. This Chapter introduces you to design techniques you can use to make your document easy to read.[1]

To see for yourself the impact design techniques have on a writer's ability to communicate, compare the two examples of Abraham Lincoln's Gettysburg Address below. First, try to read this version:

```
FOUR SCORE AND SEVEN YEARS AGO OUR FATHERS BROUGHT FORTH
ON THIS CONTINENT, A NEW NATION, CONCEIVED IN LIBERTY,
AND DEDICATED TO THE PROPOSITION THAT ALL MEN ARE CREATED
EQUAL.
NOW WE ARE ENGAGED IN A GREAT CIVIL WAR, TESTING WHETHER
THAT NATION, OR ANY NATION SO CONCEIVED AND SO DEDICAT-
ED, CAN LONG ENDURE.  WE ARE MET ON A GREAT BATTLE-FIELD
OF THAT WAR.  WE HAVE COME TO DEDICATE A PORTION OF THAT
FIELD, AS A FINAL RESTING PLACE FOR THOSE WHO HERE GAVE
THEIR LIVES THAT THAT NATION MIGHT LIVE.  IT IS ALTOGETHER
FITTING AND PROPER THAT WE SHOULD DO THIS.
BUT, IN A LARGER SENSE, WE CAN NOT DEDICATE, WE CAN NOT
CONSECRATE, WE CAN NOT HALLOW THIS GROUND.  THE BRAVE MEN,
LIVING AND DEAD, WHO STRUGGLED HERE, HAVE CONSECRATED IT,
```

FAR ABOVE OUR POOR POWER TO ADD OR DETRACT. THE WORLD WILL LITTLE NOTE, NOR LONG REMEMBER WHAT WE SAY HERE, BUT IT CAN NEVER FORGET WHAT THEY DID HERE. IT IS FOR US THE LIVING, RATHER, TO BE DEDICATED HERE TO THE UNFINISHED WORK WHICH THEY WHO FOUGHT HERE HAVE THUS FAR SO NOBLY ADVANCED. IT IS RATHER FOR US TO BE HERE DEDICATED TO THE GREAT TASK REMAINING BEFORE US, THAT FROM THESE HONORED DEAD WE TAKE INCREASED DEVOTION TO THAT CAUSE FOR WHICH THEY GAVE THE LAST FULL MEASURE OF DEVOTION, THAT WE HERE HIGHLY RESOLVE THAT THESE DEAD SHALL NOT HAVE DIED IN VAIN, THAT THIS NATION, UNDER GOD, SHALL HAVE A NEW BIRTH OF FREEDOM, AND THAT GOVERNMENT OF THE PEOPLE, BY THE PEOPLE, FOR THE PEO-PLE, SHALL NOT PERISH FROM THE EARTH.

Now read this one:

Four score and seven years ago our fathers brought forth on this continent a new nation, conceived in Liberty, and dedicated to the proposition that all men are created equal.

Now we are engaged in a great civil war, testing whether that nation, or any nation so conceived and so dedicated, can long endure. We are met on a great battle-field of that war. We have come to dedicate a portion of that field, as a final resting place for those who here gave their lives that that nation might live. It is altogether fitting and proper that we should do this.

But, in a larger sense, we can not dedicate, we can not con-secrate, we can not hallow this ground. The brave men, living and dead, who struggled here, have consecrated it, far above our poor power to add or detract. The world will little note, nor long remember what we say here, but it can never forget what they did here. It is for us the living, rather, to be dedicated here to the unfinished work which they who fought here have thus far so nobly advanced. It is rather for us to be here dedicated to the great task remaining before us, that from these honored dead we take increased devotion to that cause for which they gave the last full measure of devotion, that we here highly resolve that these dead shall not have died in vain, that this nation, under God, shall have a new birth of freedom, and that government of the people, by the people, for the people, shall not perish from the earth.

The text in both versions is identical. Which was easier for you to read? Even the most brilliant writing can get lost if it is presented poorly.

Depending on the purpose of your document, you may not have unlimited discretion in formatting your text. Court rules sometimes prescribe formatting requirements such as margin size and font. Statutes may dictate that required disclosures appear in all caps or specific font sizes.

You should follow all rules that govern the format of your document. The rules may not cover every aspect of the document's appearance, however, leaving you free to make at least some of your own design choices. In other settings, you may have greater discretion. Letters, emails, internal law office documents, and the like may be subject to formatting norms but not requirements.

Unless a rule dictates format, you should make design choices that complement the purpose of your document. Doing so increases the likelihood that your reader will, in fact, read and understand what you have written.

Choose a Legible Font

The design characteristics, size, and weight of the font you choose affect the readability of the text.

Some fonts are monospaced, meaning each character takes up the same amount of space. Most fonts are proportionately spaced, meaning each character takes up only the amount of space it needs.

```
This is a monospaced font.
```

This is a proportional font.

Do not use a monospaced font unless a court rule requires it. Monospaced fonts are harder to read because they leave too much white space between some characters.

Additionally, some fonts have serifs — little flags or feet at the ends of each letter's vertical strokes — and some are sans serif — straight-edged, without the flags. Notice the differences between these two examples:

This is a serif font.

This is a sans serif font.

Serif fonts are usually best for the body of a document, although some people prefer sans serif fonts for email and other documents that will be read on a screen. Most word processing software offers a range of serif and sans serif fonts. Be sure to choose one with a professional appearance. *Decorative fonts* are never appropriate for legal documents or professional communications.

An additional consideration in font choice is point size. Point sizes are not standard across fonts, as you can see from the following examples:

This is 12-point Helvetica.

This is 12-point Georgia.

This is 12-point Times New Roman.

Consequently, you may have to try different options for your document. For the body of most documents, the text should be between 10 and 13 points.

Most of your text should be written in a normal weight (or roman) font, but you can occasionally use *italics* or **bold** for emphasis. With serif fonts, italics generally indicate less emphasis than bold. With sans serif fonts, italics don't stand out very much, so use bold for emphasis.

Do not underline text for emphasis. It makes the text hard to read and in electronic documents may be confused with hyperlinks. ***Avoid using both italics and bold together***, and NEVER USE ALL CAPITAL LETTERS (ALL CAPS) FOR EMPHASIS. ALL CAPS ARE HARD TO READ, AND ONLINE THEY INDICATE SHOUTING.

Use the Right Amount of Space to Separate Words and Lines

The background part of a page or screen that does not contain text is called white space. The amount of white space in your document affects readability. Too little squashes the text and makes it hard to read. Too much tires the eye and interferes with the flow of reading.

To incorporate the right amount of white space, start at the sentence level. Insert only one space after punctuation, even periods.[2] When documents were produced with monospaced type on typewriters, inserting two spaces after a period helped space the text properly. With word processing software, two spaces are unnecessary and put extra white space between sentences that reduces readability.

Text alignment also affects white space. For most documents, align the text with the left margin. This keeps the proper amount of space between words, and the ragged edge on the right creates visual interest. Full justification adjusts the amount of space between words and letters to make the left and right margins even. If you use fully justified text, adjust your document settings to hyphenate words, especially if you use a monospaced font. Otherwise, words may be awkwardly spaced to create even margins. Do not center the text in the body of your document. You can, but do not have to, center short headings, as explained more fully below.

Next, consider the amount of space between lines. This is trickier than you might expect because the optimal line spacing falls between settings in most word processing software. Single spacing puts the lines slightly too close together; 1.5 lines puts them slightly too far apart. Double spacing reduces readability by spreading out the text too much.

If you are unable to adjust your document settings, you will have to evaluate the line spacing to see what looks best. Readers often prefer single-spaced documents because they are shorter and because paragraphs and headings stand out, making the structure easier to follow.

The better option, however, is changing the document settings to adjust the line spacing. Setting options vary across word processing programs, but here are two common options for adjusting line spacing:

- Use the multiple line spacing option with the value set between 1.03 and 1.24.

- Use a fixed or exact setting somewhere between 120% and 145% of the font size you are using (e.g., a 12-point font would have line spacing set at exactly 14.4 points to be 120% of the font size).

You can separate paragraphs by inserting space between them. Alternatively, you can indent the first line of a new paragraph.

Use Generous Page Margins

Margin size affects the proportion of text to white space and line length. The rule of thumb is that 50% of the page should contain text and the rest should be white space. Line length of 45 to 90 characters optimizes readability. This is why professionally printed documents like newspapers, magazines, and court opinions are often set in columns.

Legal documents rarely meet these standards, especially those with page limits or set margin specifications. But when you have the discretion to set your own specifications, use margin settings that keep the lines of text at a readable length and leave an appropriate amount of white space. Most word processing software does not offer an automatic way to calculate average line length. (Do not confuse line length measured by character count with sentence length measured by word count. Recall from Chapter 5 that most sentences should be 25 words or less, and advanced grammar checking settings will calculate average sentence length for you.) If you type a line of text and check the character count, you will see the line length and can adjust your document settings as needed.

If you must use a monospaced font, one-inch side margins will usually produce the right line length with a 12-point font size. With a 10- to 12-point proportional font, side margins set between 1.5 and 2 inches will usually do the trick.

Use Visual Cues to Orient the Reader Within the Text

Providing readers with visual cues to orient them within the text improves readability. This is especially true for documents read on a screen. In print, readers can tell whether they are at the beginning, middle, or end of a document simply by holding it and flipping the pages. Text on a device lacks these spatial cues, making it difficult for readers to figure out where they are within a document.

Headings can be effective for guiding readers through your document because they divide the text into readable sections. Too many headings, however, make the text choppy. Just as lists within lists can be confusing, multiple levels of headings and subheadings are hard to follow. You are likely dicing your text into chunks that are too small when you use more than two levels of subheadings.

As noted above, short headings can be centered. Longer headings should normally align with the body text at the left margin. The better practice is to include white space above and below headings to make them stand out. At a minimum, add white space above headings to create visual chunks of text. Putting headings in a slightly larger font than the body text visually reinforces the hierarchy of the headings.

Whenever possible, draft headings that reference the content of the text that follows. Generic headings are not as useful for orienting or guiding readers through a document's content.

Consider using scientific numbering if appropriate to your task:

1. First main heading
    1.1 First subpoint
    1.2 Second subpoint
2. Second main heading

Scientific numbering orients readers within the text better than lettered headings and subheadings (A., B., etc.) because the numbering makes the relative positions of the points and subpoints apparent.

Compare these examples:

A.   Headings

This heading states its subject but does not otherwise give any clues about the content that follows. What about headings? Designating the heading as point A indicates that it may be (but not necessarily is) a subheading within a larger main point. If it is a subheading, the reader cannot determine which main point it relates to — First? Second? Forty-fifth? Thus, the designation does not help the reader identify the point's position within the document. The heading text is the same size as the body text. Further, the heading is not surrounded by white space or properly aligned with the text below it.

1.1 How to tell if a heading is formatted properly

This heading is formatted properly. It tells the reader what to expect in the text and is surrounded by white space to make it stand out. The scientific numbering tells the reader that this is the first subpoint within the first main point of the document. The heading is in a slightly larger point size than the body text. The first letter of the heading aligns with the first letter of the text below it. It is not centered or indented further than the body text.

Pagination can also orient readers within the text. Pagination that includes the total number of pages (e.g., Page 12 of 15) especially helps readers find and keep their place in a document read on a screen.

Use Lists and Tables

Lists and tables can make complex material understandable to readers.

The list trick was described in Chapter 6. This trick works especially well in documents read on a screen because it makes individual items stand out visually for the reader. If possible, change the color of the bullet from black to gray. This will draw the reader's eye to the bulleted text instead of the bullet point itself.

Tables are good tools in two circumstances:

- to display information not easily presented in a textual paragraph, such as a series of numbers; and

- to make relationships among items visually apparent to the reader.

One useful way to present variable information is with an if-then table. One column defines the variable, and one or more additional columns list the information affected by the variable. For example, font choices for emphasizing text can be described in narrative form or with an if-then table. Compare this textual summary with the table that follows it:

Use italics for subtle emphasis with a serif font and bold for strong emphasis, but not both together. With a sans serif font, use bold for emphasis instead of italics. In neither case should you use underlining or all caps for emphasis.

IF YOUR DOCUMENT HAS THIS TYPE OF FONT	USE THESE GUIDELINES FOR EMPHASIZING TEXT
Serif font	• Use italics for subtle emphasis. • Use bold for strong emphasis. • Do not use italics and bold together, underlining, or all caps.
Sans serif font	• Use bold for emphasis. • Do not use italics, underlining, or all caps.

The textual summary is not complicated. But the if-then table with the bulleted lists makes the differences easy to see.

Tables cannot take the place of all narrative text. They work best when they complement the text. Tables with too much information do not convey meaning effectively and can overwhelm the reader. Further, the font and line spacing considerations that apply to body text apply with equal force to tables. Consider this example:

If your document has this type of font	**Use these guidelines for emphasizing text**
Serif font	• A serif font has small flags at the end of each vertical stroke. • Use a font that appears professional; avoid all decorative fonts. • Use 10- to 12-point font in most documents for body text. • Use italics for subtle emphasis. • Use bold for strong emphasis. • Avoid bold and italics together. • Do not use underlining or all caps because they are hard to read.
Sans serif font	• A sans serif font has straight vertical strokes. • Use a font that appears professional; avoid all decorative fonts. • Use 10- to 12-point font in most documents for body text. • Use bold for emphasis because italics don't stand out enough with a sans serif font. • Do not use bold and italics together for emphasis. • Do not use underlining or all caps because they are hard to read; further, underlining may be confused with hyperlinks, and all caps indicates shouting.

This table has lost its focus. The content does not align with the headings. Some bullet points include too much information to be presented effectively in table form. The lines of text in the right column are too close together. The effect is a cluttered table that is hard to read.

Special Considerations for Email

No one reads email. This is not to say we don't send and receive email. We do. But people rarely read the email they receive carefully; a good number don't even read the email they send very carefully. Of course, all of the clear writing techniques described in this book will serve you well in drafting email. Once you have drafted a well-written email, you increase the likelihood that a recipient will actually read the message if you pay attention to formatting:

- avoid special formatting;
- signal content with a clear subject line;
- use short paragraphs;
- put the most important information at the beginning;
- make critical information stand out; and
- use appropriately formal writing conventions.

Avoid any formatting that may look different to the recipient than it does to you. Lawyers often prefer to draft emails in a word processing program and paste the text into an email. This is a sound practice because it prevents the writer from sending an incomplete or ill-considered message by accident. But people access email in so many ways you cannot be sure that tabs and indents, unique fonts, special characters, and the like will appear as intended on the recipient's end. You may have the option to erase formatting or paste content as plain text to minimize formatting errors.

Include a clear subject line to signal the content of the email. A clear subject line primes the reader for the message's content. Missing, generic, and off-topic subject lines do the opposite.

Keep paragraphs short, preferably no more than three sentences and certainly no more than five. Long paragraphs are hard to read in print. They are virtually impossible to read on a phone. Single space within paragraphs, and separate paragraphs by inserting space instead of indenting to spread the text out visually.

Put the most important information at the beginning. People tend to skim email, causing them to miss information buried in the middle of a message. How many times have you asked two questions in an email, only to receive a response that answers but one of them? If you state the purpose of the message or put requests for information or action at the beginning, your recipient is more likely to see that material.

Make critical information stand out. Use bold sparingly to emphasize critical items. Use bulleted or numbered lists with care. They stand out in email and focus the reader's attention, but using them also creates some risk that the formatting will look different on the recipient's end.

Use writing conventions appropriate to the formality of the message. Although email has traditionally lacked the formality of paper correspondence, a message's appearance should reflect a level of seriousness commensurate with the communication. You know without being told, for example, that emojis and informal abbreviations (like BTW or IDK) are too casual for any professional communication and that all spelling and grammar must be correct. By contrast, using a salutation and closing makes an email appear more formal. Readers use these sorts of visual cues to assess the importance of a message, which can then affect the care with which they read it.

➢ Exercise 32

Answer the questions that follow. Then look at the answer key in the Appendix:

1. Open your word processing software. Identify the default settings for each item listed below.

   a. Font

   b. Point size

   c. Line spacing

   d. Text alignment

   e. Page margins

2. Open any document you have drafted (such as your resume or a brief or memorandum), and adjust the document settings to improve its readability, taking into account font selection, point size, line spacing, text alignment, and margins. If the document has headings or bulleted lists, format those parts of the document to conform to the guidelines in this chapter.

3. Create an if-then table explaining the rule below.

   An eligible employee, meaning one who has been employed at least 12 months by the employer and has worked at least 1,250 hours during the previous 12 months, is entitled to unpaid leave for the birth of the employee's child or the placement of a child with the employee for adoption or foster care.

Reader's Exercise Key

These are not the answers to the exercises. They are some of the many possible answers. Often a writing problem has more than one good solution. Your answer may be better than the one given here. If that happens, you should feel encouraged, not puzzled.

➤ Exercise 1

Remember that the distinction between working words and glue words is rough-hewn, and reasonable people can differ about particular words in a sentence. Thus, don't worry if your answers aren't exactly like the ones suggested here.

1. Here is the original sentence with the working words underlined:

> In point of <u>fact</u> <u>350</u> <u>grams</u> of <u>J-12</u> <u>plastic</u> <u>explosive</u>, <u>seven</u> <u>detonating</u> <u>devices</u>, and <u>one</u> <u>50-foot</u> <u>roll</u> of <u>insulated</u> <u>copper</u> <u>wire</u> were <u>discovered</u> by the <u>federal</u> <u>security</u> <u>inspectors</u> at the <u>airline</u> <u>gate</u> <u>hidden</u> on the <u>accused's</u> <u>person</u> at the <u>time</u> he was <u>detained</u> and <u>arrested</u>. (45 words total / 28 working words)

The original sentence could be revised to read:

> The <u>federal</u> <u>security</u> <u>inspectors</u> <u>discovered</u> <u>350</u> <u>grams</u> of <u>J-12</u> <u>plastic</u> <u>explosive</u>, <u>seven</u> <u>detonating</u> <u>devices</u>, and <u>50</u> <u>feet</u> of

insulated copper wire hidden on the accused's person when they detained and arrested him at the airline gate. (36 words total / 27 working words)

2. Here is the original sentence with the working words underlined:

There is nothing in the loan agreement, as we read its terms and conditions, that could be construed to allow prepayment of the loan by the borrower and simultaneous termination of the City's equity share. Prepayment of the loan will not affect the City's equity share, which will remain due upon either the sale of the property in question or upon the occurrence of any of the breaches specified in said loan agreement. (73 words total / 33 working words)

The original sentence could be revised to read:

We do not read the loan agreement as allowing a borrower both to prepay the loan and simultaneously terminate the City's equity share. Prepayment will not affect the equity share. It will remain due upon either sale of the property or occurrence of any breach specified in the agreement. (49 words / 28 working words)

3. Here is the original sentence with the working words underlined:

When entering into an agreement regarding the settlement of a claim made by a client, a lawyer must not offer or agree to a provision that imposes a restriction of the right of the lawyer to practice law, including the right to undertake representation of or take particular actions on behalf of other clients or potential clients with similar or different claims. (62 words total / 34 working words)

The original sentence could be revised to read:

In settling a client's claim, a lawyer must not offer or make an agreement that restricts the lawyer's right to practice law, including the right to represent or act for other persons. (32 words total / 20 working words)

➢ Exercise 2

1. To control how his art collection could be displayed after his death, the doctor created a very restrictive trust, hoping to keep everything exactly as it was during his lifetime.

2. Concerning the taxpayer's enormous charitable gift deduction, she did not submit an appraisal of the donated bronze sculpture. Therefore, we propose to disallow the deduction, as the Revenue Department's standard operating procedure requires.

3. The plaintiff seeks relief similar to a mandatory injunction. Before the merger of law and equity, only a court of Chancery could grant that kind of relief.

4. To raise funds, the charity's organizers held a silent auction because a game of chance would not be permitted by state gaming law.

➢ Exercise 3

1. Because parties can often find enough points of agreement to resolve a lawsuit before trial, mediation can doubtless be effective in reducing the backlog of pending cases.

2. When the court issues a scheduling order, the case will proceed to discovery.

3. After the court's ruling, the defendants filed a notice of appeal.

4. Mandatory injunctive relief is inappropriate here.

5. Although the statute of limitations has now passed, the plaintiff just filed a complaint alleging negligence.

6. You cannot begin construction until the design review committee approves the plans.

7. Usually the insurance adjuster will start by denying the claim.

8. The auditors review the files annually.

9. Because the regulations are hard to understand, inspectors issue citations for violations more often now.

10. An attorney can be disciplined for suing without a good faith belief that the claim is legally and factually sound, and both the attorney and the client are subject to litigation sanctions as well.

➢ Exercise 4

1. A person might make a significant gift to charity for three related reasons.

2. First, the person often primarily wants to help the charity.

3. Second, the person might want to avoid capital gains tax by giving the charity an asset that is now much more valuable than it was when the person acquired it.

4. Third, if the person is very wealthy, a large charitable gift can reduce the estate tax that must be paid when the person dies.

5. Tax lawyers and estate planners should show clients how their natural desire to give to charity can also reduce their taxes.

➢ Exercise 5

An agent owes a duty to the principal to act with the care, competence, and diligence that are normally exercised by agents of ordinary skill and prudence in similar circumstances. An agent's special skills or special knowledge are facts to consider in determining whether the agent acted properly. Moreover, an agent has a duty to act only within the scope of the agent's actual authority. An agent must comply with all lawful instructions from the principal (or persons previously designated by the principal) concerning the agent's actions on the principal's behalf.

➢ Exercise 6

1. A health insurer often automatically rejects a claim for coverage by a policyholder whose medical care is not preapproved.

2. Instead, the insurer should carefully consider whether the policyholder sought routine or emergency treatment.

3. Emergency treatment does not have to be preapproved. The insurer must evaluate what constitutes an emergency on a case-by-case basis.

4. In an emergency, the policyholder has to decide quickly to seek treatment and may not be able to contact the insurer.

5. Every contract — including an insurance contract — contains an implied term that the parties will deal fairly and act in good faith.

6. The insurance company is obligated to respond coherently to a policyholder's claim for emergency care that was not preapproved.

➢ Exercise 7

1. Benson <u>failed</u> [active] to renew his commercial driver's license for five years after it expired. Therefore, he <u>was required</u> [passive] to retake the exam to obtain a new license.

2. For more than three months after obtaining a new license, Benson <u>sought</u> [active] a position as a driver. Then he <u>caused</u> [active] an accident in his personal vehicle and <u>was charged</u> [passive] with reckless driving. He <u>was convicted</u> [passive] of a misdemeanor last June.

3. Last July, a new statute <u>went</u> [active] into effect. It <u>requires</u> [active] Benson to disclose the traffic conviction to any employer who hires him as a commercial driver.

4. Benson mistakenly <u>believed</u> [active] the statute did not apply to him. He <u>reasoned</u> [active] that he was not required to dis-

close the conviction because the vehicle involved in the accident was his personal car, not a commercial vehicle.

5. Benson <u>was hired</u> [passive] as a commercial driver last August. Two weeks later, he <u>was fired</u> [passive] by his employer and <u>cited</u> [passive] by the police for failing to disclose the prior traffic conviction. Benson now <u>challenges</u> [active] the disclosure statute's validity.

➤ Exercise 8

1. The statute was enacted in 2018.

   (Passive voice is appropriate here. The thing done — enacting the statute — is more important than the actor — the legislature.)

2. Neither the depositor nor anyone else notified the bank that the ATM card had been stolen.

   (The truncated passive voice in the dependent clause at the end of the sentence is proper because we don't know who stole the ATM card.)

3. An applicant must complete and submit a financial aid application to the Financial Aid office at least 90 days before the start of classes.

4. After 180 days, either party can terminate this Agreement.

5. The police discovered two kilograms of an unidentified white powder in the spare tire well of the Volvo sedan.

6. You can deduct charitable gifts of appreciated assets at their fair market value at the time of the gift, and in that way you can avoid capital gains tax.

7. The store's security guard prohibited the plaintiff from leaving the store; therefore, the plaintiff filed a claim for false imprisonment against the guard and the store owner.

> ## Exercise 9

1. In a tort case, an actor is not liable for harm that is different from the harms whose risks made the actor's conduct tortious. Likewise, an actor is not liable for harm when the tortious aspect of the actor's conduct did not increase the risk of harm. But sometimes an actor's tortious conduct causes harm to a person that, because of the person's physical or mental condition or other characteristic, is of a greater magnitude or different type than might reasonably be expected. In that event, the actor is liable for all such harm to the person. (97 words, average sentence length 24 words)

2. Americans take pride in the jury trial system, but the system has flaws. We could improve the way jurors are selected, treated in the courtroom, instructed on the law, and compensated. Recognizing this, the American Bar Association has adopted Principles Relating to Juries and Jury Trials. The document proposes reforms of our jury system. For example, it says that in civil cases, we should ordinarily allow jurors to submit written questions for witnesses. (73 words; average sentence length 15 words)

3. The law of sentencing criminal offenders should have three goals. First, sentencing should be severe enough to reflect the gravity of the offense and the blameworthiness of the offender. Second, where success is reasonably likely, sentencing should seek to rehabilitate the offender, deter future offenses, incapacitate dangerous offenders, and restore crime victims and communities. Third, sentencing should be no more severe than is necessary to achieve the first two goals. (70 words, average sentence length 18 words)

➤ Exercise 10

1. Sometimes, after a harm occurs, a litigant takes remedial measures that would have made the harm less likely to occur. That litigant's adversary cannot offer evidence of the remedial measures to prove the litigant's negligence or other culpable conduct.

2. In almost every common law jurisdiction, witnesses cannot testify until they swear or affirm that their testimony will be truthful. The oath or affirmation must be worded in a way that will awaken a witness's conscience and mind to the duty to tell the truth.

3. If a lawyer offers a client's testimony that she believes is true, but later learns that it is false, the lawyer must take "reasonable remedial measures." The first of these measures is for the lawyer to speak with the client in confidence. The lawyer should tell the client about the lawyer's duty of truthfulness to the court and should try to get the client to correct or withdraw the false testimony.

4. If the first remedial step doesn't work, the lawyer should consider withdrawing as counsel if that will undo the effects of the client's false testimony. In taking this step, the lawyer should always try to cause the least harm to the client and the client's lawful objectives. *Restatement (Third) of the Law Governing Lawyers* § 120 (2000); American Bar Association Model Code of Professional Responsibility, Rule 3.3.

5. If, and only if, the first two remedial steps fail, the lawyer must disclose the falsehood to the tribunal. That is a drastic step because it allows the lawyer, when necessary, to disclose information that would otherwise be privileged, protected by the ethical duty of confidentiality, or both.

➤ Exercise 11

1. The advance health care directive permits medical treatment to be discontinued in any of the following circumstances:

   - an individual has an incurable and irreversible condition that will result in her death relatively soon; or
   - an individual becomes unconscious and, to a reasonable degree of medical certainty, will not regain consciousness; or
   - the likely risks and burdens of treatment outweigh the expected benefits.

2. A health care provider will not withhold or withdraw treatment from a patient unless the patient signs an advance directive giving contrary instructions.

3. The following health care providers must comply with the patient's instructions regarding continuation of treatment:

   - nurses; and
   - doctors; and
   - physician's assistants; and
   - nurse practitioners; and
   - emergency medical technicians.

4. A homeowners' association that is chartered by South Carolina must act within the limits set by the following:

   - its own charter; and
   - the Constitution and laws of South Carolina; and
   - the Constitution and laws of the United States of America.

   Within those limits, the association has the implied power to make reasonable rules to govern use of the members' common property.

➤ Exercise 12

1. The builder said that only the smoke detectors complied with the new building code.

   ("Only" could fit in several places in this sentence, depending on the intended meaning.)

2. This sentence has at least two possible meanings:

   The court's opinion ignores the privacy policy updates adopted after the data breach.

   or

   The privacy policy was adopted after the data breach. The court's opinion ignores the updates to the privacy policy.

3. Counsel argued that the plaintiff was subjected to retaliation by his supervisor and then constructively discharged.

4. Finding that the defendant was a flight risk, the judge refused to release her on bail.

5. The Department of Agriculture intended the new dairy regulations to reduce the open-air discharge of methane gas.

➤ Exercise 13

1. Conflicts of interest can seriously erode, if not entirely destroy, the relationship of trust between attorney and client. One attorney's conflict is usually imputed to all the other attorneys in the law firm.

2. One type of conflict of interest occurs when an attorney enters into any kind of business transaction with a client. That is a conflict even if the transaction is profitable for everyone. But the attorney can solve the conflict by making adequate disclosures.

3. The terms of the transaction must be fair and reasonable to the client. The attorney must disclose the terms to the client in writing, using clear, plain language.

4. a. procedures for docket management in multi-district litigation

   b. research for the argument for preemption based on the Commerce Clause

   c. patent application for the medication to treat coronary artery disease

   d. restrictions on clients' disbursement accounts

➤ Exercise 14

1. An attorney is allowed to reveal a client's confidential information to prevent serious financial injury due to a crime the client is about to commit or to prevent death or serious bodily injury.

2. You can impeach a witness with a prior criminal conviction if it was a misdemeanor that involved dishonesty or false statement or if it was a felony.

3. A corporation is liable for an investor's financial losses due to the criminal conduct of an officer or employee if that person was both (a) high-ranking, and (b) acting within the scope of his or her authority.

➤ Exercise 15

1. To make the small-loan market more efficient in Central America, we need to find better ways for lenders to share information on defaults by borrowers without encouraging lenders to restrain trade by agreeing among themselves on interest rates and risk assessment.

2. When you as a lawyer come into the possession of your client's property in connection with a matter, you must keep that

property separate from your own property. If the property is money, you must put it into a trust account in the state where your offices are located (or in a different state if your client consents). If the property is something other than money, you must identify it as belonging to your client, and you must put it in a safe place that is appropriate to its size and nature.

3. The defendant corporation set out to lie to people who own little and who have little scientific knowledge. To earn more profits for itself, the defendant used false advertising, hoping to convince these people that antiretroviral drugs cause impotence and that the defendant's vitamin pills are better than antiretrovirals in combating HIV.

4. a. A judge may examine witnesses who were called by the parties, and the judge may also call witnesses whom the parties have not called.

    b. A prosecutor may sometimes inveigle a judge to call a hostile but essential witness whom the prosecutor herself needs but fears to call. Questioning such a witness from the bench often diminishes the witness's hostility and makes the witness more useful.

    c. Because patients may claim that their treatment fell below the standard of medical care, a doctor must maintain a malpractice insurance policy.

➤ Exercise 16

1. a. In *Simpson v. Union Oil Co.*, Justice William O. Douglas said, but did not prove, that: "The patent laws which give a seventeen-year monopoly on 'making, using, or selling the invention' concern the same general subject as the antitrust laws, and the two should be construed together. The patent laws modify the antitrust laws to some extent. That is why General Electric was decided as it was."

b. Cecilia Wickham, Esq., entered her appearance for the plaintiff, and defendant Augustine Crowell entered his appearance on his own behalf.

2. a. We urge the court to consider the arguments in favor of the motion to dismiss the complaint.

 b. We submit that the oral statement in question is admissible in evidence over hearsay objection.

3. As a trial lawyer, you are subject to local court rules. These concern efficient court administration, such as what size paper to use for court documents. You are also subject to the preferences of individual judges, such as whether you are to sit or stand when questioning a witness. But most important, you are subject to the rules of legal ethics that apply in court proceedings. For example, you must not take a frivolous legal position — one that you cannot support under the current law or by a good faith argument for changing the law. Likewise, you must not state your personal opinion about the justness of a cause, the culpability of a litigant, or the credibility of a witness, and you must not make legal arguments that are not supported by evidence in the record.

4. a. The prosecution stated its objection to the motion to suppress.

 b. The court issued its opinion on the qualified immunity defense.

 c. The corporation failed to notify its shareholders about the inventory losses.

 d. All drivers involved in an accident must provide their insurance information.

5. a. The plaintiff described her injuries to the jury.

 b. The plaintiff described his injuries to the jury.

 c. The plaintiff described their injuries to the jury.

➢ Exercise 17

1. a. From 1776 until the end of the War of 1812, the overriding

   subject   verb
   question was whether the nation could survive.

   b. During those formative years, the subject weakest of the three

   verb
   branches of government ~~being~~ [was] the judiciary.

   (*Being* cannot be used by itself as a verb to form a complete sentence. It has to be joined with another form of *to be* to function properly as a linking verb — am being, was being, are being, etc.)

   c. Not particularly brightening the outlook, the President's

   subject   helping verb (added)
   appointment of John Marshall to the Court in 1801, [was]

   verb
   unenthusiastically supported even by the Federalists.

   d. Under John Marshall's guidance, the subject   verb Court consolidated

   verb
   far-reaching judicial power and put Congress's authority on

   a broad and permanent constitutional footing.

2. a. independent clause   dependent clause
   The Jeffersonians were certain that the Constitution was a
   dependent clause, cont.   dependent clause
   limiting document and that John Marshall was a malignant
   dependent clause, cont.
   force.

   b. independent clause
   They charged the Chief Justice with usurping power, and
   independent clause
   they further charged him with converting his colleagues to
   independent clause, cont.
   his plans for aggrandizement.

   c. independent clause
   The Federalists, on the other hand, expected the Court to
   independent clause, cont.
   consolidate national power and contain the emerging forces
   independent clause, cont.
   of democracy.

➢ Exercise 18

1. At least one precedent exists for nonjudicial action by allies against a former enemy leader whose acts seem abhorrent, and that precedent is the case of Napoleon.

   (This sentence consists of two independent clauses, so it needs a comma and the conjunction *and*.)

2. Napoleon escaped from exile in Elba, and he marched again on Europe.

   (The sentence is correct as written. It consists of two independent clauses joined by the conjunction *and*, with a comma inserted before the conjunction.)

3. Representatives of all the European states except France declared Napoleon beyond the law and had to resolve the question of what to do about him.

   (This sentence contains one subject with two verbs and does not need a comma.)

4. The Prussians said to shoot him, but the Russians advocated more delicately for summary execution.

   (This sentence consists of two independent clauses joined by the conjunction *but*; it needs a comma before the conjunction.)

➢ Exercise 19

1. After Napoleon escaped from Elba came renewed calls for his execution.

   (This sentence is correct as written. The introductory element is followed by inverted word order, so it doesn't need a comma.)

2. Having condemned the execution of Louis XVI, the European leaders would have been embarrassed to execute Napoleon.

   (Use a comma after an introductory element.)

3. To punish Napoleon for his actions, the leaders resolved to exile him to St. Helena.

(Use a comma after an introductory element.)

4. Upon exile Napoleon was out of the way and kept at British expense.

(This sentence is correct as written. A short introductory element doesn't require a comma.)

➤ Exercise 20

1. a. Lutz, who sued Reliance Nissan for wrongful termination, could not show that the arbitration clause in her employment contract was unconscionable.

   (The *who* clause is nonrestrictive. It adds information about Lutz but is not necessary for the sentence to make sense. Thus, it is set off with commas.)

   b. Conversely, the plaintiff who successfully challenged the arbitration clause produced evidence of unconscionability.

   (The sentence is correct as written. The *who* clause is restrictive because it identifies which plaintiff, so it is not set off with commas.)

   c. The evidence of unconscionability, which was overwhelming, persuaded the court to decide the two cases differently.

   (The *which* clause is nonrestrictive. It adds information about the evidence but is not necessary for the sentence to make sense. Thus, it is set off with commas.)

   d. The opinion states, among other things, that unconscionable contracts are not enforceable.

   (The phrase *among other things* is a parenthetical element that is set off with commas.)

   e. Lutz argued that she entered into the contract under duress; however, the court was not persuaded.

(*However* is used here as a transitional word connecting two independent clauses. It must be preceded by a semicolon and followed by a comma.)

f. To explain its ruling, therefore, the court distinguished Lutz's case from the earlier case.

(*Therefore* is used here as a transitional word in the middle of a sentence. It must be set off with commas.)

2 a. The defendant's motion, which asked the court to dismiss the complaint, was not served properly.

(Use *which* here because the clause is set off with commas, indicating that it is a nonrestrictive clause adding information about the motion.)

b. The motion that the court granted was not dispositive.

(Use *that* here because the clause is not set off with commas, indicating that it is a restrictive clause identifying the motion.)

c. The corporation that employs the defendant may be vicariously liable for her actions.

(Use *that* here because the clause is not set off with commas, indicating that it is a restrictive clause identifying the corporation.)

d. The plaintiff intends to rely on res ipsa loquitur, which is a tort law doctrine.

(Use *which* here because the clause is set off with a comma, indicating that it is a nonrestrictive clause adding information about res ipsa loquitur.)

➤ Exercise 21

1. Patents protect novel and nonobvious inventions, including medicines, tools, innovative processes, and machines.

   (Insert commas to separate a series of connected items. Use the Oxford comma to separate the last two items to clarify that innovative modifies only processes, not machines.)

2. Patents encourage innovation by protecting novel, nonobvious inventions.

   (*Novel* and *nonobvious* are coordinate adjectives that both modify *inventions*, so they are separated by a comma.)

3. Copyrights protect original works of authorship, such as books, including comic books and graphic novels; music; and artwork, including drawings and paintings.

   (The series of items protected by copyrights contains internal commas, so the items are separated by semicolons.)

4. Making an unauthorized copy of an original movie soundtrack is unlawful.

   (The sentence is correct as written. *Original* and *movie* are not coordinate adjectives; *original* modifies *movie soundtrack* and should not be followed by a comma.)

➤ Exercise 22

1. The defendant began serving his sentence on November 10, 2017, at the federal correctional facility in Anthony, Texas.

   (The year and the state are set off with commas.)

2. The engineering report by Sandra Ellison, Ph.D., concluded that "the design was structurally sound."

   (The title is set off with commas. The quotation is integrated into the sentence, so it is not introduced with a comma.)

3. The judge told the witness, "Please answer the question."

   (The quote is introduced with a comma.)

4. The witness said she "saw the defendant clearly."

(The sentence is correct as written. The quote is incorporated into the sentence, so it is not introduced with a comma.)

➤ Exercise 23

1. On May 25, 2018, Melissa Stanton sued Oak Valley Associates, the building contractor, and the janitorial company.

2. Stanton alleges that she lives in Valdosta, Georgia.

3. Heritage Corporation is the janitorial company that serves Oak Valley Associates. Medical Facility Construction is the building contractor and is owned by Arthur Marshall, M.D.

4. The complaint, which was filed exactly four years after Stanton was injured, alleges ordinary negligence, gross negligence, and recklessness.

5. The defendants argue that the complaint was filed too late; therefore, they move to dismiss.

6. The three-year statute of limitations applies, defendants argue, because the plaintiff's complaint seeks damages for personal injuries.

7. Stanton was in a long-term care facility for more than a year after the injury and argues that the statute of limitations was tolled while she was incapacitated.

8. Because she was incapacitated, Stanton was unable to pursue her claim.

9. The defendants, however, challenge that assertion.

10. Stanton's injuries include persistent tooth pain, which began immediately after she fell; jaw pain, which was exacerbated by a later injury in the long-term care facility; and headaches.

➤ Exercise 24

1. The appellate judges asked why the trial court ruled the way it did.

   (The sentence is correct as written. It is an indirect question that requires a period, not a question mark.)

2. Did the trial judge err by excluding the evidence?

   (The sentence is a direct question that requires a question mark.)

3. Recovery for intentional infliction of emotional distress requires conduct that causes an average member of the community to exclaim, "Outrageous!"

   (An exclamation point is appropriate because the rule requires a display of strong emotion.)

➤ Exercise 25

1. Our economic system depends in part on legal recognition of property rights; parties must be able to enforce their property rights when necessary.

   or

   Our economic system depends in part on legal recognition of property rights, and parties must be able to enforce their property rights when necessary.

   (This sentence consists of two independent clauses. They can be joined with a semicolon if no conjunction is used. If they are joined with a comma, the coordinating conjunction *and* must be inserted.)

2. Attorney conflicts of interest can arise in many settings; therefore, you must check for conflicts before accepting any new case.

(This sentence consists of two independent clauses joined with the transitional word *therefore*. The transition must be preceded by a semicolon and followed by a comma.)

3. The defendant is charged with horizontal price fixing, which is an antitrust offense; breach of contract in the sale of the business; and fraud, which is a common-law tort.

(This sentence contains a series with internal commas, so the items are separated with semicolons.)

4. A motion to dismiss is filed before a responsive pleading; a motion for judgment on the pleadings is filed after the answer is filed.

(The sentence is correct as written. It consists of two independent clauses that are closely related, so they can be joined with a semicolon.)

➤ Exercise 26

1. Rule 12 provides that the following defenses must be raised by motion before a responsive pleading: lack of subject-matter jurisdiction, lack of personal jurisdiction, and improper venue.

(Use a colon to introduce a series.)

2. Judge Learned Hand was quoted as saying, "If we are to keep our democracy, there must be one commandment: thou shalt not ration justice."

(Use a colon within the quotation to introduce an elaboration. Note that the comma used to introduce the quotation is correct because the quotation is one sentence.)

3. As Eleanor Roosevelt said: "People grow through experience if they meet life honestly and courageously. This is how character is built."

(Use a colon to introduce a quotation longer than one sentence.)

➤ Exercise 27

1. The proposed change to the tax law affects these groups: (a) married filers who have been deducting state and local taxes from their federal returns, (b) both married and single filers who have been deducting interest on home equity loans, and (c) single filers who have been claiming the earned income tax credit.

   (Use parentheses to tabulate the items in the series.)

2. The Joint Committee on Taxation (JCT) is charged with investigating the operation and effect of internal revenue taxes. The JCT (a nonpartisan committee established by the Revenue Act of 1926) calculated the effects of the proposed change.

   (Use parentheses in the first sentence to introduce the acronym. Use them in the second sentence to set off explanatory material.)

3. The proposed change will affect any taxpayer eligible to file as a head of household (as set out in the statute).

   (Use parentheses to clarify that *as set out in the statute* modifies *head of household*, not *proposed change*.)

➤ Exercise 28

1. Sewage sludge—the substance at issue in this case — differs from solid waste.

   (Use em-dashes to set off the material that interrupts the sentence.)

2. Farmers recognize the benefits — economic, ecological, and agricultural — of using disinfected sewage sludge for agricultural purposes.

   (Use em-dashes instead of hyphens to set off the material that interrupts the sentence.)

3. The ideal time to use disinfected sewage sludge is during the May–July growing season.

(The sentence is correct as written. The en-dash indicates a date range.)

➤ Exercise 29

1. Sewage sludge is a by-product of wastewater treatment that includes biosolids. It is generally a solid or quasi-solid mud-like substance, typically consisting of water and 2–28% [*or* from 2% to 28%] solids.

(*Sewage sludge* is a compound term that is not hyphenated. *By-product* is a compound term that is hyphenated. *Biosolids* is a term that is not hyphenated. The prefix *quasi* is ordinarily followed by a hyphen. *Mud-like* is a single modifier. The percentages indicate a range and can be separated either by an en-dash or by the words *from . . . to*.)

2. The state's environmental law categorizes any treated wastewater containing less than twenty-eight percent solids as sewage sludge.

(*Twenty-eight* is a compound number that requires a hyphen.)

3. The judge did not wish to appear hard hearted in sentencing the defendant.

(The sentence is correct as written. *Hard hearted* is not hyphenated because it follows the term it modifies.)

4. The public may criticize judges who are either especially soft- or hard-hearted jurists.

(*Especially* is not followed by a hyphen because it is an adverb that ends in -ly. *Soft-hearted* and *hard-hearted* are hyphenated because each is a single modifier, but the common element only has to be used one time.)

➤ Exercise 30

1. Good legal writing requires no hereinafter's or whereinbefore's.

   (The sentence is correct as written because *hereinafter* and *whereinbefore* are referred to as words.)

2. Justice O'Connor's concurring opinion took issue with the majority's reliance on cases from the 1920s, before the expansion of Congress's power under the Commerce Clause. Hers is the more persuasive of the two opinions.

   (*O'Connor, majority,* and *Congress* are possessives formed with *'s*. The plural of 1920 does not require an apostrophe. The possessive *hers* does not use an apostrophe. The plural *opinions* does not use an apostrophe.)

3. A business's net worth is not always a good measure of its future profitability.

   (Business is a possessive formed with *'s*. Its, when used as a possessive, does not contain an apostrophe.)

4. Alice's and Ted's fathers-in-law purchased the property together.

   (Both Alice and Ted need apostrophes to form possessives because two different people — the father-in-law of Alice and the father-in-law of Ted — purchased the property. The plural of father-in-law is fathers-in-law with no apostrophe.)

➤ Exercise 31

1. The most common causes of attorney discipline are alcohol and greed.

2. Defense counsel sat in silence; the evidence was admitted without objection.

3. The one-year statute of limitations has made our deadlines shorter. I don't like its effect because it's created a hectic work environment.

4. We should listen to our instincts when assessing a legal argument's validity.

5. Lay witnesses can be paid for their expenses and time lost from work; however, a lay witness's request for additional payments cannot be granted.

6. Justice Ginsburg quoted Sarah Grimké: "I ask no favor for my sex. All I ask of our brethren is that they take their feet off our necks."

7. In a premature appeal from the trial court's order, the plaintiff raises various meritless arguments.

8. The judge instructed counsel, "Call your next witness please."

9. The Department of Labor (DOL) advises employers concerned about compliance to follow the safe harbor provisions (Parts 1–3 of the regulations).

10. The plaintiff's attorney — leaping to his feet — shouted, "Objection!"

➤ Exercise 32

1. This question has no set answer. The point is simply for you to familiarize yourself with your word processor's default settings. Often you will want to change some or all of these settings, depending on the document you are drafting.

2. This question has no set answer. The point is simply for you to see with your own work how document settings affect readability.

3. Here is one possible way to format an if-then table for the rule:

IF YOU ARE AN EMPLOYEE WHO HAS:	THEN YOU ARE ENTITLED TO UNPAID LEAVE FOR:
• Worked for the same employer for at least 12 months; and • Worked at least 1,250 hours in the previous 12 months.	• The birth of your child; or • The care of an adopted or foster child placed with you.

Chapter Endnotes

Chapter 1

1. David Mellinkoff, *The Language of the Law* 23 (Boston, Little, Brown 1963).

2. *Mylward v. Welden* (Ch. 1596), reprinted in C. Monro, Acta Cancellariae 692 (London, William Benning and Co. 1847). Joseph Kimble has pointed out that the person who wrote, and subsequently wore, the offending document may have been the plaintiff's son, a nonlawyer. Professor Kimble dryly notes that the son was probably following a lawyer's form. Joseph Kimble, Plain English: *A Charter for Clear Writing*, 9 Cooley L. Rev. 1, n. 2 (1992), relying on Michele M. Asprey, *Plain Language for Lawyers* 31 & n. 26 (Federation Press 1991).

3. Letter to Joseph C. Cabell (Sept. 9, 1817), reprinted in 17 *Writings of Thomas Jefferson* 417–18 (A. Bergh ed. 1907).

4. The Plain Writing Act of 2010, Pub. L. No. 111–274, 5 U.S.C. § 301 note, specifies that "each agency shall use plain writing" in new or substantially revised documents. Federal regulations are also required to be written in plain, clear, and understandable language. Executive Order 12866 (Sept. 29, 1993); Executive Order 12988 (Feb. 5, 1996); Executive Order 13563 (Jan. 18, 2011). That this requirement has to be restated periodically suggests that the effort to draft plain language regulations is ongoing.

5. The provision demanding user's souls was an April Fool's Day prank. *7500 Online Shoppers Unknowingly Sold Their Souls*, Fox News Tech, http://www.foxnews.com/tech/2010/04/15/online-shoppers-unknowingly-sold-souls.html (Apr. 15, 2010). Payment with firstborn children was inserted as an experiment by a security firm. Rachel Feltman, *Londoners accidentally pay for free Wi-Fi with a firstborn, because no one reads anymore*, The Washington Post, https://www.washingtonpost.com/news/speaking-of-science/wp/2014/09/29/londoners-accidentally-pay-for-free-wi-fi-with-a-firstborn-because-no-one-reads-anymore/?utm_term=.f5fee-04b0ab9 (Sept. 29, 2014).

6. This is partly how Cambridge Analytica and other companies obtained Facebook users' personal data. Elizabeth Dwoskin & Tony Romm, *Facebook's rules for accessing user data lured more than just Cambridge Analytica*, The Washington Post, https://www.washingtonpost.com/business/economy/facebooks-rules-for-accessing-user-data-lured-more-than-just-cambridge-analytica/2018/03/19/31f6979c-658e-43d6-a71f-afdd8bf1308b_story.html?utm_term=.da6932e1300d (Mar. 19, 2018). Other examples in the consumer context include being locked into long-term contracts, being unable to return merchandise, and being unable to change or cancel travel reservations. Rebecca Smithers, *Terms and conditions: not reading the small print can mean big problems*, The Guardian, https://www.theguardian.com/money/2011/may/11/terms-conditions-small-print-big-problems (May 11, 2011); *see also* Ansgar Koene, *Never read the terms and conditions? Here's an idea that might protect your online privacy*, The Conversation, http://the conversation.com/never-read-the-terms-and-conditions-heres-an-idea-that-might-protect-your-online-privacy-62208 (July 15, 2016).

7. This premise is taken from David Mellinkoff, *The Language of the Law* vii (Boston, Little, Brown, 1963); see also David Mellinkoff, *Dictionary of American Legal Usage* vii (West 1992).

8. *Palsgraf v. Long Island R. Co.*, 248 N.Y. 339, 162 N.E. 99 (1928). Professor Wydick selected *Palsgraf* as an example because it

is familiar to all who have studied law. In general, however, Justice Cardozo's writing style is too ornate for modern tastes. For good examples of modern plain English style, examine the opinions of United States Supreme Court Justice Elena Kagan or former United States Circuit Judge Richard Posner.

Chapter 2

1. The distinction between working words and glue words is neither profound nor precise, and reasonable people can disagree about whether a given word in a sentence is a working word or a glue word. If the distinction is helpful to you, use it as a tool, but don't think it's scientific or sacred. Other scholars have made similar distinctions in the functions of different types of words. See Steven Pinker, *The Language Instinct* 117–120 (William Morrow & Co. 1994) (differentiating content words that carry meaning from function words that are "scaffolding for the sentence"); see also Robert A. Chaim, *A Model for the Analysis of the Language of Lawyers* 33 J. Legal Educ. 120 (1983); Randolph Quirk, Sidney Greenbaum, Geoffrey Leech, and Jan Svartvik, *A Comprehensive Grammar of the English Language* 67–75 (Longman 1985).

2. Many of the ideas in this section originated in Amy E. Sloan, *Two Rules for Better Writing*, 38 Md. B.J. 57–58 (Sept./Oct. 2005).

3. This prescription is part of a "Paramedic Method" devised by Professor Richard A. Lanham for rendering first aid to sick sentences. *See* Richard A. Lanham, *Revising Prose* x (5th ed. Longman Pearson 2006); *see also* Joseph M. Williams, *Style: Toward Clarity and Grace* 27–40 (Univ. of Chicago 1995).

4. *See* Bryan A. Garner, *A Dictionary of Modern Legal Usage* 294–297 (2d ed., Oxford 1995); David Mellinkoff, *Mellinkoff's Dictionary of American Legal Usage* 129–32 (West 1992). They may also be called doublets and triplets. *Federal Plain Language Guidelines* 38–39 (Rev. 1 May 2011); Antonio Gidi & Henry Weihofer, *Legal Writing Style* 76–80 (West Acad. Pub. 3d ed. 2018).

5. *See* Peter M. Tiersma, *Legal Language* 10–17 (Chicago 1999); David Mellinkoff, *The Language of the Law* 38–39, 121–22 (Boston, Little, Brown 1963).

6. Tiersma, *Legal Language* at 13–15.

7. Garner, *A Dictionary of Modern Legal Usage* at 294.

8. *Id.* at 294, 640. The three terms *ordered, adjudged,* and *decreed* once had slightly different meanings, but Garner says that the single term *ordered* will usually suffice. *Id.* at 625.

9. *See* Fed. R. Evid. 801(c); *McCormick on Evidence* §§ 246–51 (John W. Strong gen. ed., 7th ed. West 2014).

10. David Mellinkoff notes that a few coupled synonyms have become so "welded by usage" that they act as a single term. These few are tolerable, he says, when used in the proper context. Mellinkoff, *Mellinkoff's Dictionary of American Legal Usage* at 129–32. For example, *pain and suffering* is acceptable in tort pleadings, and *full faith and credit* is acceptable in a brief or opinion on that constitutional clause.

11. Bryan Garner says that *last will and testament* is a ceremonial phrase that does no harm when used as the title of a client's will. But, Garner says, if you were writing a brief or an opinion about someone's will, you should call it just plain *will*, not *last will and testament*. See Garner, *A Dictionary of Modern Legal Usage* at 296–97, 516.

Chapter 3

1. C. Edward Good, *Mightier Than the Sword*, 44–45 (Blue Jeans Press 1989) (derivative noun); Joseph M. Williams, *Style: Toward Clarity and Grace*, 29–36 (U. Chicago Press 1995) (nominalization); *Federal Plain Language Guidelines* 23 (Rev. 1 May 2011) (hidden verb); Helen Sword, *Zombie Nouns*, The New York Times, https://opinionator.blogs.nytimes.com/2012/07/23/zombie-nouns/ (zombie noun) (Jul. 23, 2012) (zombie noun).

2. Amy E. Sloan, *Two Rules for Better Writing*, Md. B.J. 57–58 (Sept./Oct. 2005).

3. *Federal Plain Language Guidelines* at 23.

Chapter 5

1. *Federal Plain Language Guidelines* 50 (Rev. 1 May 2011).

2. The history of the long, long sentence is told in David Mellinkoff, *The Language of the Law* 152–70 (Boston, Little, Brown 1963); *see also* Peter M. Tiersma, *Legal Language* 55–59 (Chicago 1999); David Mellinkoff, *Legal Writing: Sense & Nonsense* 58–60 (West 1982).

3. As quoted in Ernest Gowers, *The Complete Plain Words* 166–67 (1st U.S. ed., revised by Sidney Greenbaum and Janet Whitcut, published by David R. Godine 1988).

Chapter 6

1. For more specific guidance, *see* Bryan A. Garner, *Guidelines for Drafting and Editing Court Rules*, 169 F.R.D. 177, 190–94 (1997); *Federal Plain Language Guidelines* 56 (Rev. 1 May 2011).

2. *See* Reed Dickerson, *The Fundamentals of Legal Drafting* 115–24 (2d ed. Boston, Little, Brown 1986).

3. *Handling Vertical Lists*, Get It Write http://www.getitwrite online.com/archive/101406VerticalLists.htm (2006).

4. *Id.*

Chapter 7

1. For a similar list of all-purpose fuzz words, see Ken Smith, *Junk English* 36 (Blast Books 2001).

2. 17 U.S.C. § 102 (2012).

3. Aristotle, *Rhetoric* 1404b, in 11 *The Works of Aristotle* (W. Ross ed. 1946).

4. 1 U.S.C. § 1 (2012).

5. Alison Frankel, *Pronouns matter: SDNY judge opts for plurals in case with genderqueer plaintiff*, Reuters, https://www.reuters.com/article/otc-frankel-pronoun/pronouns-matter-sdny-judge-opts-for-plurals-in-case-with-genderqueer-plaintiff-idUSKBN1I24DH (May 2018); Jessica Bennett, *She? Ze? They? What's in*

a Gender Pronoun? The New York Times, https://www.nytimes.com/2016/01/31/fashion/pronoun-confusion-sexual-fluidity.html (Jan. 2016).

6. *The Chicago Manual of Style*, 5.48 (17th ed. U. Chicago Press 2017). *The Associated Press Style Book and Briefing on Media Law* 292 (Basic Book 2017).

7. *See* Theodore Bernstein, *Miss Thistlebottom's Hobgoblins* 116–18 (Farrar, Straus, and Giroux 1971); Henry W. Fowler, *A Dictionary of Modern English Usage* 579–82 (2d ed. revised by Sir Ernest Gowers, Oxford 1965).

8. Henry W. Fowler, *The New Fowler's Modern English Usage* 736–38 (3rd ed. edited by R.W. Burchfield, Oxford 1996); Allan M. Siegal and William G. Connolly, *The New York Times Manual of Style and Usage* 312 (Times Books 1999); *The Associated Press Style Book and Briefing on Media Law*, 292–93 (Basic Books 2017).

9. Joseph M. Williams, *Style: Toward Clarity and Grace* 187 (Univ. of Chicago 1995).

Chapter 8

1. The history of the use (and nonuse) of punctuation in the law is interesting. You can learn more about it from David Mellinkoff, *The Language of the Law* 152–70 (Boston, Little, Brown 1963). Other sources with information on this topic include: David Mellinkoff, *Legal Writing: Sense & Nonsense* 57 (West 1982); Richard Wydick, *Should Lawyers Punctuate?*, 1 Scribes J. of Leg. Writing 7 (1990); Joseph Robertson, *An Essay on Punctuation* 1–14 (1785), reproduced in facsimile, *English Linguistics 1500–1800*, No. 168 (Scolar Press 1969); Robert Peters, *A Linguistic History of English* 298–99 (Houghton Mifflin 1968); Simon Daines, *Orthoepia Anglicana* 70–73 (London 1640), reproduced in facsimile, *English Linguistics 1500–1800*, No. 31 (Scolar Press 1967); *see also* Barbara Strang, *A History of English* 104–55 (Methuen Pub. 1970); Mindele Treip, *Milton's Punctuation and Changing English Usage* 1582–1676,

14–53 (Methuen Pub. 1970); Percy Simpson, *Shakespearian Punctuation* 7–15 (Clarendon 1911).

2. The choices are legion and include the following: Bryan A. Garner, *The Redbook: A Manual on Legal Style* (4th ed. West Acad. Pub. 2018); *The Chicago Manual of Style* (17th ed. Chicago 2017); Allan M. Siegal & William G. Connolly, *The New York Times Manual of Style and Usage* (5th ed. Times Books 2015); Frederick Crews, *The Random House Handbook* (6th ed. McGraw-Hall 1991); Lynn Quitman Troyka & Douglas Hesse, *Simon & Schuster Handbook for Writers* (11th ed. Pearson 2017); *The Bluebook: A Uniform System of Citation* (20th ed. 2015); Coleen M. Barger, *The ALWD Guide to Legal Citation* (6th ed. Wolters Kluwer 2017).

3. This dedication is likely apocryphal, but it illustrates nicely the problem that omitting the Oxford comma can create. Arika Okrent, *The Best Shots Fired in the Oxford Comma Wars*, Mental Floss, http://mentalfloss.com/article/33637/best-shots-fired-oxford-comma-wars (Jan. 22, 2013).

4. The case is *O'Connor v. Oakhurst Dairy*, 852 F.3d 69 (1st Cir. 2017). After the First Circuit ruled that the missing comma rendered the statute ambiguous, the parties settled the suit. John McCoy, *Oakhurst Dairy's $5M Settlement Driven by Grammar Rules*, Bloomberg Law News, https://www.bna.com/oakhurst-dairys-5m-n57982088598/ (Feb. 9, 2018). The language in the example is an edited version of the statute at issue in the case.

Chapter 9

1. As noted in Chapter 8, note 2, you have many good choices: Bryan A. Garner, *The Redbook: A Manual on Legal Style* (4th ed. West Acad. Pub. 2018); *The Chicago Manual of Style* (17th ed. Chicago 2017); Allan M. Siegal & William G. Connolly, *The New York Times Manual of Style and Usage* (5th ed. Times Books 2015); Frederick Crews, *The Random House Handbook* (6th ed. McGraw-Hall 1991); Lynn Quitman Troyka & Douglas Hesse, *Simon & Schus-*

ter Handbook for Writers (11th ed. Pearson 2017); *The Bluebook: A Uniform System of Citation* (20th ed. 2015); Coleen M. Barger, *The ALWD Guide to Legal Citation* (6th ed. Wolters Kluwer 2017).

2. Coleen M. Barger, *ALWD Guide to Legal Citation* (6th ed. Wolters Kluwer 2017); *The Bluebook: A Uniform System of Citation* (20th ed. 2015).

3. Bryan A. Garner, *Guidelines for Drafting and Editing Court Rules*, 169 F.R.D. 176, 195 (1997).

4. Bryan Garner, *The Redbook: A Manual On Legal Style* 1.57 (4th ed. West Acad. Pub. 2018); *The Chicago Manual of Style*, 6.78 (17th ed. U. of Chicago Press, 2017).

Chapter 10

1. This chapter provides introductory guidance for presenting text effectively, not comprehensive instruction in document design. If this is a topic that interests you, other resources that delve into document design in greater detail include Matthew Butterick, *Typography for Lawyers* (2d ed. O'Connors 2015), https://typographyforlawyers.com; Bryan Garner, *The Redbook: A Manual On Legal Style* (4th ed. West Acad. Pub. 2018); Ruth Anne Robbins, *Painting with Print*, 2 J. ALWD 108 (2004); Mary Beth Beazley, *Writing (and Reading) Appellate Briefs in the Digital Age*, 15 J. App. Prac. & Process 47 (2014); Derek H. Kiernan-Johnson, *Telling Through Type: Typography and Narrative in Legal Briefs*, 7 J. ALWD 87 (2010); and *Requirements and Suggestions for Typography in Briefs and Other Papers*, from the United States Court of Appeals for the Seventh Circuit, http://www.ca7.uscourts.gov/forms/type.pdf (last accessed July 5, 2018). Many of the ideas in this chapter come from these sources.

2. Although some people continue to put two spaces after a period, typographers agree that one space is the better practice. Matthew Butterick, *Typography for Lawyers* 41–44 (2d ed. O'Connors 2015); see also Bryan Garner, *The Redbook: A Manual On Legal*

Style (4th ed. West Acad. Pub. 2018). A recent study suggested that two spaces create more readable text. But the study tested a monospaced font read on a screen, and it found only a modest (3%) increase in reading speed among readers who already habitually put two spaces after a period. Matthew Butterick, *Are Two Spaces Better Than One? A Response to New Research*, https://practicaltypography .com/are-two-spaces-better-than-one.html (accessed July 5, 2018).

Index